W0035892

03
A U I D series

AUID series presents texts extracted from the final doctoral dissertations of the Doctoral Program in Architectural Urban Interior Design (AUID) at Politecnico di Milano, Department of Architecture and Urban Studies.

Editor
Francesca Zanotto
Graphic Design
Francesco Trovato

AUID Head
Alessandro Rocca

AUID Scientific Board
Guya Bertelli, Marco Biraghi, Marco Borsotti, Marco Bovati, Margitta Buchert, Pier Federico Caliari, Simona Chiodo, Luigi Cocchiarella, Emilia Corradi, Valentina Dessì, Andrea Di Franco, Immacolata C. Forino, Roberto Gigliotti, Matthias Graf von Ballestrem, Andrea Gritti, Laura Montedoro, Carles Muro, Marco Navarra, Filippo Orsini, Orsina Simona Pierini, Gennaro Postiglione, Alessandro Rocca, Alessandro Rogora, Pierluigi Salvadeo, Luigi Spinelli, Ilaria Valente

POLITECNICO
MILANO 1863

DIPARTIMENTO DI ARCHITETTURA
E STUDI URBANI
DEPARTMENT OF ARCHITECTURE
AND URBAN STUDIES

AUID series

These agile booklets document the research carried out within our doctoral program. We decided not to publish the entire doctoral works, which are extensive and articulated, but to, instead, select and extract, from those scientific concentrates of sophisticated knowledge, the most comprehensible studies that are obviously associated with themes of the current debate on architectural design. These texts have, therefore, been forcibly stripped of their premises, of the state of the art and apparatus overview. They have, at times, even been disconnected from the broader rationale they belonged to. Hence, it is an arbitrary and, sometimes, unjust process, if we consider the scientific coherence of the original constructs. However, dear reader, we assure you that it was done with the best of intentions, an effort aimed at building a small, solid and well-designed bridge between the elite world of academic research and the fluid, open and permeable to discussion, updates of the critical evolution of contemporary architectural design.

Alessandro Rocca

The author would like to express her sincere gratitude to her supervisors, Prof. Luca Basso Peressut and Prof. Francesca Lanz, without whom this research would not have been possible. The author is also thankful to all professors of the AUID program and to her family for their constant support.

–

This book presents an elaboration of selected materials from the author's doctoral thesis, *Dissonant Memories in the Post-Soviet Space: Newly Established Museums and Political History in Russia (1991–2016)*, supervised by professor Luca Basso Peressut and co-supervised by professor Francesca Lanz. The thesis was successfully defended on June 30th, 2020, at the Department of Architecture and Urban Studies, Politecnico di Milano.

ISBN 978-88-6242-544-5

First edition January 2022

© LetteraVentidue Edizioni
© Maria Mikaelyan

LetteraVentidue Edizioni S.r.l.
Via Luigi Spagna 50 P
96100 Siracusa, Italy

www.letteraventidue.com

Maria Mikaelyan

The Museum as a Political Instrument

Post-Soviet Memories and Conflicts

LetteraVentidue

Contents

9 Foreword
Luca Basso Peressut

11 Multidimensional Memory:
In Search of a Theoretical Framework

27 Post-Soviet Memories and Conflicts:
A Multilayer Museum Mapping

45 Museum and Exhibition Design
as Political Instruments

78 Notes

94 Bibliography

Foreword

Luca Basso Peressut

Museums have always been places of *narration* and *representation*: narration of stories, artworks, and artifacts, whose representation takes place through the exhibition design and architecture. The forms of architecture here become an expression of the values of a society and the values of the age. Museums are connected to social, political, and cultural changes. Thus, they are subject to reformulations of meaning and role over time, and thereby to transformative dynamics aimed at actualizing their messages and discourses. Museums cannot be limited to accumulating collections but must continually redesign the narrative matrix that holds together the care of heritage, cognition, and evolving knowledge. For instance, significant questions arise today with regard to the interpretation of facts that belong to the recent past, such as the wars and political events of the last century. These are often painful or traumatic issues over which different individual and collective visions and memories collide. To describe these issues, it is necessary to activate an idea of culture seen as a practice of exchange, participation, and creativity. The answers given in the museum field are a manifestation of the political and cultural choices of nations, communities, and local groups. But above all, they must be the result of the ability of those who design the contents, spaces, and forms of communication (historians, museologists, architects, and exhibition designers) to innovate, going beyond the limits of established languages.

Multidimensional Memory: In Search of a Theoretical Framework

The theoretical conceptualization of the dimension of memory throughout different fields of contemporary academic research is rooted in the late 1970s and 1980s when the awareness of the Holocaust and other mass extermination crimes grew in the West. A number of significant Holocaust-related public issues across Europe and America began to draw attention to questions concerning individual, social and collective memory, and to their role in public commemoration and monumentalization of the past. National and international debates in both continents on the NBC miniseries *Holocaust* (broadcast in 1978–1979), which became the most widely viewed television show on this topic of all time[1], establishment of the special commission on the Holocaust by United States president Jimmy Carter in 1978, the crucial discussion between the West German right-wing and left-wing intellectuals on the historicization of the Third Reich and the Holocaust in the late 1980s[2] are among these questions. Finally, a historiographical and cultural "memory turn" in France became an important catalyst for the subsequent global dissemination of the discourse on national memory studies that had originated from Pierre Nora's multi-volume series *Les lieux de mémoire* (1984–1992)[3] and his perception of cultural memory as collective remembrance within national frameworks.

Nora suggested the concept of preserving historical memory through the actualization of its objects – museums and collections, monuments and memorials, cemeteries and sculptures, holidays and anniversaries, etc. Using these realms of memory, the nation not only preserves knowledge about significant personalities and events but also unites people in a solid community. According to Nora:

> *Lieux de mémoire* are simple and ambiguous, natural and artificial, at once immediately available in concrete sensual experience and susceptible to the most abstract elaboration. Indeed, they are *lieux* in three senses of the word – material, symbolic, and functional. Even an apparently purely material site, like an archive, becomes a *lieu de mémoire* only if the imagination invests it with a symbolic aura[4].

The opposing concept of "non-sites of memory" (*les non-lieux de la mémoire*[5]) was suggested by Claude Lanzmann in 1986 to describe the abandoned sites of Nazi mass extermination in Poland, which he filmed in the 1970s. The absence of traces is directly related here to the absence of memory and thus to potential oblivion.

In his approach to memorial practices, Nora is following the path of Maurice Halbwachs who introduced the notion of "collective memory" – a pluralistic reconstruction of the past, regarding which a particular social group (ethnic, gender, professional, etc.) establishes consensus in light of the present. For Halbwachs collective memory is not a network of individual minds but the result of constant social interaction:

> One cannot in fact think about the events of one's past without discoursing upon them. But to discourse upon something means to connect within a single system of ideas, our opinions as well as those of our circle. [...] In

this way, the framework of collective memory confines and binds our most intimate remembrances to each other[6].

Another important concept within the realm of contemporary mnemonic studies is that of "social memory" deriving from Karl Mannheim's analysis of the sociology of knowledge and further explored by Peter Burke[7], Jeffrey K. Olick, and Joyce Robbins[8]. Social memory is malleable but maintains its continuity; it involves the creation of narratives that are inextricably linked to sociopolitical and economic circumstances, identitarian dynamics, and ideological trends.

Starting in the 1990s, German scholars Jan Assmann and Aleida Assmann began to develop Halbwachs's approach to "collective memory" and its subsequent derivatives into an influential concept of "cultural memory": it is seen as a present-day interpretation of meanings from the distant past transmitted through such mnemonic carriers as texts, images, or rituals[9]. "Cultural memory" is counterposed to fluid and shifting "communicative memory", which is based on interpersonal communication and thus exists within the typical framework of a three-generation cycle. National monuments, as well as public museums, are seen by Assmanns as memory sites in which "cultural memory" is transmitted down through generations with the ultimate purpose of shaping cultural identity[10]. In several publications, Aleida Assmann highlights the risks of distortion and instrumentalization related to the transition between individual and cultural memory[11].

The political and social will at multiple levels is a significant factor in this process:

> One of the reasons why memories are so complex is that they are differently constructed on the levels of individual, family, society, and nation. These levels may exist in mutual indifference, but they may also produce dissent and friction, and collide in counter-constructions. An important insight here is that top-down strategies and bottom-up movements reinforce each other[12].

The emergence in 1980s Germany of a new "culture of remembrance" (*Erinnerungskultur*) based on empathy for the victims of the Holocaust and the recognition of the collective guilt which falls on German society of today and of future generations[13], has now expanded beyond ethnic or national boundaries: methodological nationalism has been challenged by the concept of "transnational memory" unfolding across real or imagined borders[14]. On the other hand, the new cultural paradigm suggests new modes of relation between history and memory on a family level. Thus, Marianne Hirsch introduces the notion of "postmemory"– a retrospective second-generation remembrance shaped by powerful narratives of historical witnesses. According to Hirsch, «[...] postmemory is distinguished from memory by generational distance and from history by deep personal connection»[15].

Both Hirsch[16] and Assmann[17] stress the distinctive role of trauma in individual and collective remembrance: a difficult, traumatic past «[...] often has the present in its grip. In such cases, it is not we who possess it, but it that possesses us»[18]. The role of suggestive affects will grow more pronounced as society continues to be haunted by traumatic postmemory, which is often neglected, unmirrored, or ideologically manipulated within public sites of memory, primarily in memorials and museums. Perception of this social phenomenon and its place in the theoretical framework of contemporary memory studies appears to be essential for a critical analysis of museums dealing with political history in today's Russia[19].

Geopolitical transformations in Europe in the late 1980s and early 1990s have triggered the interest of scholars, journalists, photographers, and writers in abandoned sites of trauma[20], especially in Eastern Europe. Nora's and Lanzmann's concepts of sites and non-sites of memory have been further developed in various fields of studies including memory, heritage, and museum studies. Thus, M. Tumarkin suggests the term "traumascapes" to describe specific places distinguished by overwhelming legacies of violence that are remembered and continuously re-experienced with time[21]. Since the early 1990s, a wide range of similar concepts related to the topography of remembrance has been suggested, for instance, "memoryscape"[22], "heritagescape"[23], or "contaminated landscape"[24]. Following Tumarkin, who accentuates the materiality of sites where traumatic events have occurred, Patrizia Violi introduces the notion of "trauma site museums": transformed into museums, these places «[...] maintain a real spatial contiguity with the trauma itself; [...] the demonstration of such a continuity is an essential part of their inherent and constructed meaning, not to say the very reason for their existence»[25].

The spatial approach has also been applied by Rob van der Laarse[26] in his pivotal concept of "terrorscapes" featuring *in loco* historical traces of state-perpetrated violence. Due to their significant affective nature, these spaces are susceptible to different forms of memorialization, transformation, or oblivion and thus are able to communicate diverse narratives of memory[27]. "Terrorscapes" demand specific museological and museographic strategies to prevent nationalist or revisionist controversy, along with a lack of understanding by younger generations.

An important contribution to the museological conceptualization of traumatic and controversial past has been made by Sharon Macdonald, an Honorary Professor of Cultural Anthropology at the University of York. Macdonald's methodology is based on the notion of the museum as «an analytical locus for anthropology, sociology and cultural studies»[28]. During the 2000s, she develops the concept of "difficult heritage"[29], where heritage is perceived as both a material and a discursive entity. Difficult, contentious heritage is embodied in histories which are important for today's public concern but are also «[...] contested and awkward for public reconciliation with a positive, self-affirming contemporary identity»[30]. Museum displays of this kind of heritage imply multiple dilemmas, for instance, whether or not conventional boundaries may be challenged, whose memories and what narratives should be prioritized, or how the incorporation of unsettling memory within the museum space will affect heritage providers facing the challenges of post-trauma changes. On the other hand, production and exposure of competing views of the past – the «object lessons in power», to use the terminology of Tony Bennett[31] – help society constructs its culture through learning and reflection. As Macdonald states, «[a]ny museum or exhibition [...] is a theory: a suggested way of seeing the world. And, like any theory, it may offer insight and illumination»[32]. Public engagement with comparative memory discourse, which embraces sociocultural discomfort and avoids nationalist rhetoric, is capable of improving social solidarity, reconciliation, and the spirit of democracy[33].

Another significant element of the current study's methodological approach is the notion of dissonance as applied to the musealization (or museumification[34]) of political history in post-Soviet Russia. It draws on the concept of "dissonant heritage" coined by John E. Tunbridge and Gregory J. Ashworth[35]. Dissonance is understood here as a lack of public agreement or consonance, which in turn requires interventions to restore the consistency of collective identities. According to Tunbridge and Ashworth, the phenomenon of a dissonance appears when the heritages possessed by society «[...] no longer conform to the present goals of the heritage creation exercise, because they contain messages that are dissonant in the context of the prevailing norms and objectives or in terms of the dominant ideology»[36]. Accordingly, this definition has been used to set the framework of the present research: a continuous shift in political, socioeconomic, and cultural models observed in Russia since the dissolution of the USSR together with – particularly since the first presidency of Vladimir Putin – the intensification of a deliberate ideological agenda within the state politics of memory over the last decade[37], allow the concept of "dissonant memories" to be applied to the critical analysis of contemporary Russian museums focusing on political history.

However, since the opening of new frontiers in heritage and memory studies during the 1980s and 1990s, the vocabulary of shared memories related to difficult and contentious pasts has considerably expanded. Thus, Sharon Macdonald[38] reflects on "unsettling memories": previously excluded and then reincorporated in the public discourse, they undermine the already established and validated accounts of the past. Anna Cento Bull and Hans Lauge Hansen[39] propose the notion of both reflexive and dialogic "agonistic memory" that seeks to embrace various politicized representations of the past. Rob van der Laarse[40] uses the term "concurrent memories" stressing the failure of mnemonic reconciliation in Europe, as well as the existing ambiguity between victims and perpetrators, particularly common in the post-Soviet region. Finally, Tea Sindbæk Andersen and Barbara Törnquist-Plewa[41] apply the term "disputed memories" to describe the current situation in Central, Eastern, and South-Eastern Europe where the fall of old political régimes has resulted in the radical reversal of memories. Such a reversal may potentially lead to either a public reconciliation or a burst of extreme nationalist sentiment. The latter process is often encountered in the post-Soviet space. However, any of the above-mentioned notions may to some extent be applied to contemporary museum practice relating to political history in post-Soviet countries.

After the dissolution of the USSR in 1991, fifteen newly independent states had to face not only extensive socioeconomic and political changes but a total reconsideration of their national history, memory, and cultural heritage. Consequently, this resulted in contradictory arguments, misperceptions, and in some cases, ideological bias. During the last thirty years, various types of identities – from micro-identities of small social groups to national ones – were formed in the post-Soviet region, requiring new forms of interpretation, transmission, and intermediation between them. A drastic overturning of their value systems together with a lack of meaningful discourse on the construction of collective social memory or "remediation"[42] of difficult histories related to the Soviet era have brought contemporary society in post-Soviet countries, especially Russia, to contradictory world views and conflicting ideologemes[43].

The Russian state continued to live in the era of the

Yeltsin presidency characterized by openness, pluralism, and democratization across all the realms of public and individual life. Among the declared Russian Federation's national targets concerning its sociocultural politics were «[...] the preservation and development of the national culture», as well as «[...] preservation of the historical traditions and authentic living environment of various ethnic and ethnic-cultural population groups, especially minority indigenous peoples [...]»[44]. However, once applied to the realities of a vast, multi-ethnic, and multi-denominational[45] country facing post-imperialistic issues related to both internal and external colonization[46], along with the political and financial turmoil of the transitional post-Soviet period, this official cultural and identitarian agenda has had a different implementation.

By the end of the 1990s, after a decade of post-Soviet "privatization" of the country, which until then ignored the notion of property, a decade of moral disorientation, aesthetical and intellectual devaluation of all cultural concepts, Russian society was neither capable of deliberate collective reflection on its traumatic histories and memories, nor of redefining of its national self-image. In 1997, Kathleen Parthé, an expert in Russian cultural studies, claimed that the Russian national identity remained tied to the "cognitive maps" of the past – that of the spiritual Holy Rus and imperial Great Russia: «Both types of cognitive maps [...] mark strong binary contrasts between one's own and alien, and both emphasize the concept of organic wholeness, of indivisibility (*tsel'nost'*) as crucial to Russian national identity and security»[47]. According to Daniil Dondurei, it occurred because Russian intellectuals did not offer any ideological support for the political and socioeconomic models of modernization during the post-Soviet years – they «[...] did not realize the need for a cultural reset. And thereby rejected systemic project-based thinking»[48].

Since Vladimir Putin's re-election to the presidency for a third term in 2012, issues related to the shaping of official memory and its interaction with other categories of social memory[49] have gained considerably more importance in Russian society than in the previous post-Soviet years. Shifting towards a more conservative, nationalist political and ideological model, and therefore progressively reviving neo-imperial rhetoric[50], Putin's administration has intensified the process of nationalization of historical memory, especially in terms of the Soviet past. This process had already been activated in the mid-2000s with the rise of the World War II Soviet victory cult[51]. According to Dina Khapaeva, a scholar specializing in post-Soviet cultural studies, construction of the war myth has had an important impact on the Russian collective memory: «The most important function of the war myth (which it has successfully fulfilled into the present day) is to assure [Russians] that the Gulag remains just a minor episode in a heroic Soviet history»[52]. Moreover, it has become a turning point in the complex relationship between civil society and the political class: for the first time after the dissolution of the USSR, Russian politicians have started to see Soviet history as one of the instruments of ideological manipulation. As Nikolai Svanidze, a member of Russia's Presidential Council for Civil Society and Human Rights, stated:

> History is important to the authorities not as a science, not as the truth about the past. In this sense, it is absolutely insignificant to them. It is important precisely as political, ideological support. And therefore, the average voter should know about history exactly as much as the authorities need him to know, and only what authorities want him to know[53].

The intensification of ideological bias in the field of memory can clearly be seen after the annexation of Crimea in 2014 and the subsequent military conflict in East Ukraine, considered by a number of authors[54] as the end of the post-Cold War international order. Along with the failure of the bill *On Counteracting the Rehabilitation of Crimes of Stalin's Totalitarian Regime* in the Russian parliament in 2015 and 2016, and tensions surrounding the Perm-36 Memorial Museum and the Memorial NGO[55], an evident manipulation of public opinion concerning political repression has been taking place over recent years. In July 2017, the state-owned Russian Public Opinion Research Center (VCIOM) published a survey on political repression carried out under Stalin[56], where 43% of respondents claimed to see mass repression as a necessary measure that allowed Stalin to ensure order within society[57]. Shortly after, in October 2017, VCIOM published another survey, shifting the focus from the whole period of the Great Terror to the 1930s and 1940s: 53% of its respondents saw the victims of political repression as «innocent people», and 36% claimed to see perpetrators as guided by national interests[58]. Such a discrepancy between two almost contemporaneous surveys accentuated the existing memory-related dissonance among different social groups and fostered distrust between the political class and society.

Following the idea of Reinhart Koselleck[59] that involvement in committed crimes is vital for the sense of national responsibility, the author considers the present dissonance regarding collective memory as a matter of serious concern for today's Russian society. The transformation of history into an instrument for the transmission of political propaganda is not only exacerbating the divisions within society but could possibly lead to a memory-related crisis of Russian national identity.

Another example of sociocultural dissonance inherent in today's Russia can be seen in the coexistence of dispersed symbolic violence (e.g., censoring of the *Nureyev* ballet at Moscow's Bolshoi Theater, under the pretext of illegal homosexual propaganda among minors, and the subsequent criminal investigation of its director Kirill Serebrennikov[60]) and potential "affects of victimhood"[61]: Putin's political régime identifies itself as a "victim" of alleged enemies (external and internal forces that are constantly trying to destroy the Russian state, its national identity, culture, etc.), which are nothing but a visionary projection created by the "victim" itself. The régime is declaring the need to defend the nation[62] but, according to philosopher Mikhail Iampolski, this need lies «[...] not in the political field, but in the field of cultural chimeras that can be neither defeated nor tamed»[63], and hence opens the way for further identity-related issues in today's Russian society.

Post-Soviet Memories and Conflicts: A Multilayer Museum Mapping

One of the main purposes of the present research is to select, gather and critically analyze a wide range of primary and secondary sources which constitute the basis for further scientific research in the fields of museum studies, cultural politics, and memory studies. The museological framework of the research offers a concise overview of the museological state of affairs in the post-Soviet space, based on the available primary and secondary source data.

Proceeding from a quantitative to a qualitative approach, a detailed multilayer mapping comprises Russian museums and memorials that focus on political history and contentious heritage, and that have been established *ex novo* during the past three decades. The first-layer mapping reveals the complex and multi-pronged character of the contemporary museological situation in the former Soviet Union. A thorough study of available primary sources – national statistical reports or data retrieved directly from the websites of state statistical services – shows a significant increase in the number of museums during the twenty-five years following the dissolution of the USSR: from 2 571 in 1991 to 5 125 in 2016[1]. Concurrently, total museum attendance, marked by a distinct decrease around 2000 (from 164,1 to 108,8 mln visits per year), enjoyed a recovery. However, in 2016 there was only a slight increase in comparison to 1991: from 164,1 to 176,7 mln visits per year[2].

Returning to the number of newly established museums, calculation of the growth rates in each country (except for Turkmenistan, which has not disclosed official statistical data since 2014) gives an average result of about 100%: almost all post-Soviet countries have doubled the number of their museum institutions[3].

Shifting the analytical lens from a quantitative to a qualitative scale, the author has applied the filter of newly established post-Soviet art and history museums that are relevant on a national scale: these institutions are seen as significant for the museological process of the period under review, they feature valuable museum collections, adequate financial investments, a significant sociocultural and mediatic impact, relevant scientific activity and catchment area size. Among them are national museums, contemporary art centers, history museums, etc. The author adopts the qualitative filter in order to discard from the mapping process museums that do not adopt a scientific historical-critical approach but conduct their activities solely in terms of tourism and leisure[4].

The category of institutions dealing with the difficult and traumatic Soviet past is represented by the highest number of museums, thereby highlighting the fundamental importance of these issues for the majority of society in each country formed after the dissolution of the USSR on the one hand and, on the other hand, an active engagement of national political elites in Soviet-related public commemoration and remembrance. By representing multi-pronged, challenging, sometimes conflicting or competing narratives of political history, adopting divergent approaches to museological and curatorial practices and showing a large variability of architectural and exhibition design solutions – from austere «discarding of all forms and decisions»[5] to stylistic pastiche and aesthetic *épatage* – these museums embody the complexity of representational practices, sociocultural politics, and ideological trends in today's post-Soviet region.

After applying a series of objective and critical filters during the process of multilayer mapping of post-Soviet museums, the author decides to proceed with selection, by applying another critical filter – museums of the Russian Federation.

The decision to apply a geographic criterion and to focus research on the museological state of affairs of a specific post-Soviet country derives from the complexity of the political, socioeconomic, and cultural context in the post-Soviet space. Despite the apparent commonness of dissonant memories and contentious heritage related to the Soviet past, it is not feasible to speak about common cultural politics or similar approaches to collective memory issues in different post-Soviet countries. The discursive consistency of the Soviet federal project has been lost with the dissolution of the USSR. The same happened to the historical, ideological, cultural unity of the "Soviet people", a model that was supposed to unite various ethno-national groups into a common society, – it had unequivocally failed[6], and there is no chance for any form of this unity in the foreseeable future. Thus, an attempt to draw comparisons between the museological state of affairs in different post-Soviet countries, or between their rhetorical and narrative strategies addressing dissonant memories may lead today to inconsistent and ambiguous results.

The decision to opt for Russia as the main research area stems from several causes. Firstly, its museological tradition dates from the beginning of the 18th century, when the first public museum collections modeled on the European cabinets of curiosities started to appear in Russia[7]. Secondly, the geographic location of Russia at the boundary between Europe and Asia suggested its natural mission to incorporate and unify the Eastern and Western cultural traditions since the beginning of the 19th century[8]. Thirdly, and most importantly for the present research, the case of post-Soviet Russia has been chosen because it represents a specific and multipronged museological situation distinguished by a broad range of architectural and exhibition design concepts, narrative strategies, and rhetoric implemented in various state and private museums (as well as museums with hybrid state/private financing models), featuring collections that focus on political history. Along with the constantly increasing number of Russian museums during the last two decades[9], the spectrum of tangible and intangible heritage subject to musealization is becoming broader resulting in the wider implementation of integrated and multidisciplinary approaches to museum development[10]. Furthermore, the particularity of Russian museological situations in the field of political history consists of a strong engagement by non-governmental actors, such as private foundations, NGOs, social communities, or individual activists, even though this engagement has fallen considerably in recent years as a result of pressure from state authorities[11].

Moreover, since 2012, Russian society has remained in a boundary situation: availing itself of a moral protest against the manipulation of power by the existing political regime, it demands the new ethos, a shift in existing moral and ethical norms. It is not yet clear how and when these demands will be met. But it can be argued that this process would reshape the identitarian self-awareness of Russian society, bringing a new dimension to the perception of collective memory, and subsequently creating new narratives of museum display related to the dissonant Soviet past. Thus, the examination of today's boundary situation through the case studies of Russian museums dealing with political history and contentious heritage may also represent a fruitful avenue for future scientific investigation.

After the application of a geographic criterion, the mapping of Russian national-scale institutions established *ex novo* after 1991 and dealing with political history and contentious heritage features ten museums that are represented below.

The foundation of the Perm-36 Memorial Museum of the History of Political Repression and Totalitarianism (hereinafter referred to as the Perm-36 Memorial Museum) was one of the few attempts in Russia during the 1990s to display and interpret its

31

difficult Soviet past through the medium of a fully-fledged museum[12]. Due to its historical significance, scale, and state of conservation, the Perm-36 site has also provided a unique opportunity for the reuse of a Gulag facility for museological purposes. The former Perm-36 corrective labor colony (official abbrev. "ITK-36", later – "VS-389/36") situated in Kuchino village, in the Perm Region (Molotov District during Soviet times) of the Russian Federation, is a prime example of a Gulag detention facility that "survived" Khrushchev's de-Stalinization program and remained operative from 1946 until its closure in 1988 instigated personally by Mikhail Gorbachev.

Due to its harsh detention regime, the Perm-36 colony hosted a great number of political prisoners considered extremely dangerous to public security[13]. The situation has not changed much since Stalin's death. On the contrary, an additional special security zone was arranged in 1980, in order to provide even harsher conditions for political convicts and "repeat offenders"[14].

In 1995, the Russian Memorial NGO, in cooperation with local historian and activist, Victor Shmyrov, launched a project of the Perm-36 Memorial Museum. In 1996, the museum was opened to the public under Shmyrov's direction. Even though the site was the only Gulag camp that remained practically intact after the dissolution of the Soviet Union[15], it suffered considerable deterioration in subsequent years, when a psycho-neurological hospital was located on the site. One of the barracks and the system of barbed wire fences were demolished; other buildings were abandoned, falling into disrepair[16]. Restoration of the Perm-36 continued until 1998, with major support from various American and European non-profit organizations[17].

The buildings remained after the closure of the Perm-36 camp underwent various restoration and recovery phases. However, neither a clearly articulated methodological apparatus nor governmental policies specifying valuation, restoration, conservation, or budgeting principles and norms for the architecture of difficult and contentious heritage sites were developed in national architectural and museological practice. As a result, several buildings on the site of the only preserved Gulag camp in post-Soviet Russia are still under threat of demolition. It is important to remember that the Perm-36 Memorial Museum belongs to the "widespread museum" type (*museo diffuso*)[18] that evolves continuously and remains in strong symbiosis with the surrounding territory. Any intervention related to an architectural component of this kind of museum should be part of an integrative, multipronged, rigorously structured long-term project – a project, which is extremely sensitive to material and immaterial historical traces and, at the same time, consistently addresses the future.

The Memorial Museum NKVD Remand Prison in Tomsk is a branch of the Tomsk Regional Museum. It is situated in the basement of the 19th-century building where an internal prison of the Tomsk

OGPU-NKVD[19] regional department was located from 1923 to 1944. The museum was legally established in 1989 by the Tomsk section of the Memorial NGO. In 1993, the basement of the building was granted by the city authorities to the Tomsk Regional Museum. The Memorial Museum NKVD Remand Prison as one of its branches was opened to the public on May 25, 1996. The exhibition area of 200 sqm includes reconstructed period rooms (prison corridor, a cell for detainees in remand custody, and the investigator's office), as well as permanent themed displays. Original documents of investigative cases, embroideries, paintings, drawings, playing cards, photographic albums, wood and stone crafts made in camps and prisons are on display.

Andrei Dmitrievich Sakharov (1921–1989)[20], a distinguished nuclear physicist, Nobel prizewinner, developer of the Soviet hydrogen bomb, and one of the most famous dissidents of his time, died on December 14, 1989. Soon after, in January 1990, the Public Commission for the Preservation of Andrei Sakharov's Legacy – an NGO managing the academician's archive – was created on the initiative of his wife, Elena Bonner, and colleagues. In 1994, the Moscow City Government provided two buildings under a rent-free arrangement until 2021 to host the Andrei Sakharov Museum and Public Center Peace, Progress, Human Rights (Sakharov Center since 2012) and the academician's archive. The city authorities decided to accommodate the future museum in the late 19th-century

2-story mansion that had previously been part of the Usachev-Naydenov stately home.

A complete reconstruction of the building was carried out by Grigory Efimovich Sayevich between 1995 and 1996. Even if the internal structure of the building has been substantially altered to accommodate a wide range of functional needs (exhibition spaces, a library, multiple offices and meeting rooms, etc.), the intervention can be assessed as a well-calibrated "adaptive reuse"[21]: it has had a moderate impact on the historical identity of the building, especially in comparison to the commonplace Russian practice of demolition, complete rebuilding, or inaccurate reconstruction of architectural heritage employed during the 1990s and 2000s[22].

The Memorial Complex of the Victims of Repression in Nazran, the former capital of the Republic of Ingushetia, opened on February 23, 1997, on the anniversary of the deportation of more than 493 000 Chechens and Ingush from the Northern Caucasus to Central Asia[23]. The architectural project of the museum by M. Polonkoev is a conglomerate of nine towers entangled in barbed wire and chains. The towers replicate ancient stone battle towers inherent to Northern Caucasus vernacular architecture and symbolize nine deported ethnicities. The permanent exhibition includes several displays representing forcible mass deportation in the USSR, as well as the *In Memory of the Tragic Events of 1992* display dedicated to the Ossetian-Ingush interethnic conflict. In 2014, an adjunct display was opened outside the museum building featuring an authentic train used for the deportation of the Ingush in 1944. Visitors can enter one of the freight wagons with a small display of documents and artifacts arranged inside.

The Museum of the Katyn Memorial Complex is situated in the Smolensk region, on the site of the Katyn massacre[24] carried out under the direct orders of J. Stalin. According to Soviet archival documents and the results of numerous exhumations, in April–May 1940, around 22 000 Polish citizens (officers, civil servants, policemen, etc.) were executed by NKVD in the Katyn Forest[25]. In 1996, after the signing of a special bilateral agreement between the Russian Federation and Poland[26], construction of the memorial complex began. On July 28, 2000, it was opened under the official name of Memorial Complexes in the Burial Grounds of Soviet and Polish Citizens – Victims of Totalitarian Repression in Katyn (Smolensk Region) and Mednoe (Tver Region). The part of the memorial constructed by the Polish government consists of the Polish military cemetery. The Russian part remained essentially neglected until 2017, when, in the framework of the federal program *Culture of Russia (2012–2018)* signed by Vladimir Putin, a new museum building was inaugurated. The controversy, which has been constantly kept alive by the Russian government since 2012, can be witnessed at the entrance to the Russian part of the memorial, where the following inscription reads: "Here rest over 8 000 Soviet and over 4 000 Polish citizens".

Even today, after decades of international historical and forensic research and the publication of NKVD documents relating to the Katyn massacre, the Russian government refuses to accept the magnitude of the mass murder of Polish prisoners of war by the Soviet authorities. The same political strategy has been applied to the permanent exhibition *Russia and Poland. The XXth Century. Pages of History* of the museum, which represents numerous historical narratives – from the 1917 Revolution and 1919–1921 Polish-Soviet war to personal histories of Soviet citizens who were also victims of political repression – except the scientifically reconstructed chronology of the Katyn massacre[27].

In July 2001, the Moscow Department of Culture established the State Cultural Institution of the City of Moscow GULAG History State Museum, which is known today under the name of GULAG History Museum[28]. The initiative to create the institution was originally taken by prominent Russian historian and victim of the Soviet Gulag system, A. V. Antonov-Ovseenko, who then became the museum's first director. In 2004, the museum opened to the public and presented its first permanent exhibition in the 18th-century Petrovka Street building in the historical center of Moscow. The museum has often been criticized by the professional community from the perspectives of museology, museography, and historical narration. In 2009, prominent Russian art and architecture historian G. Revzin described the museum as awkward and strange, highlighting an excessive theatralization inherent in its exhibition design and narrative representation[29].

In 2011, the Moscow Department of Culture begins to work on expanding the museum. The total amount of 147 mln rubles (circa 3,6 mln euros) was allocated by the Moscow Department of Culture[30] for the architectural recovery and reuse of the early XXth-century building, which took place between 2013 and 2015. Since its inauguration in October 2015, the new GULAG History State Museum has a total floor area four times larger than before[31] featuring spaces for temporary exhibitions, storage rooms, offices, and meeting rooms, an auditorium, a library, and an archive.

The Memorial to the Victims of Repression of the Balkar People in the capital of the Kabardino-Balkar Republic, Nalchik, was inaugurated on March 8, 2002, on the anniversary of the 1944 deportation of more than 37 000 Balkars to Central Asia[32]. The museum project by M. Z. Guziev features a monumental mausoleum with an elongated octagonal dome, often used in the region's Islamic architecture. The imitation of the dry-stone technique, typical of Balkar vernacular architecture, is used for both the exterior and interior of the building. Originally, the Memorial had to be called The Memorial to the Victims of Political Repression and Genocide of the Balkar People, but the words "genocide" and "political" were removed shortly before its opening causing widespread public debate[33].

We may conclude that, when it comes to critical evaluation of contentious Soviet past, Russian authorities seek to adopt a conciliatory tone and language, which however contributes to controversy and ideological bias around these histories.

The Akhmad-Hadji Kadyrov Museum is dedicated to the memory of a former president of the Chechen Republic A. Kadyrov. During the 1990s, Kadyrov served as Chief Mufti of the unrecognized Republic of Ichkeria. In 2000, he was dismissed by the then Ichkerian president A. Maskhadov and decided to turn himself over to the federal authorities. Soon after, Putin appointed him chief of the Chechen administration, and in 2003 he was elected president of the Chechen Republic within the Russian Federation. On May 9, 2004, he was killed by a bomb blast during the public demonstration at Grozny stadium. On May 8, 2010, a Memorial Complex of Glory Named After A. A. Kadyrov dedicated to the Soviet victory in World War II and also to the former president was inaugurated in Grozny.

The museum, with a 40 m golden obelisk above it, is the central compositional and semantic element of the complex. Red granite is used for the exterior cladding, while the interior space is a sumptuous, extravagant composition of decorative elements made of various types of marble, plaster, or covered with gold. The permanent display showing photographs, documents, and items related to Kadyrov's death has the title *He Left Undefeated*, which is an excerpt of the speech delivered by Vladimir Putin in memory of the Chechen leader. Thus, the exhibition narrative highlights Kadyrov's loyalty to the federal center in the last years of his life, as well as his legitimacy reaffirmed by the Russian president. The architectural and exhibition design project of the museum appears to be a culmination of the ideological glorification of political leadership in contemporary Russian museological practice.

The Museum for the History of Political Repression in Inta, a medium-sized town in the Komi Republic, is a branch of the Inta Regional Museum. Opened in 2014, it represents the most valuable museological project of difficult heritage in the region, whose history is closely connected to the Soviet repressive system[34]. The museum is located in a 55 m brick water tower designed by a Swedish detainee of the Inta Mining camp (Minlag), A.-G. Tamvelius[35], in cooperation with engineers I. P. Rayskiy and B. N. Alentsev, and constructed by Gulag prisoners in 1954. The tower remained in use until the 1990s. In 2000, it was listed as a historical monument of regional importance. The architectural reuse project and the exhibition design by the TRI Group bureau transform the tower's interior into a multilevel exhibition space. The museographic itinerary unfolds along the spiral staircase leading to the upper level. Permanent displays on the lower level, which represent the town's urban development and the history of its water tower, and a *Windows to the Past* display on the upper level featuring reconstructed elements of the Minlag camp, reveal an indivisible wholeness between the architectural heritage of Inta and the heritage related to its contentious past.

The Boris Yeltsin Museum inaugurated in November 2015, is situated in Yekaterinburg, the capital of the Sverdlovsk region and the home region of the first president of the Russian Federation. The museum is part of the Boris Yeltsin Presidential Center (hereinafter referred to as Yeltsin Center) and is the property of the similarly named NGO founded in 2009, in accordance with the federal law *On Centers for the Historical Legacy of Presidents of the Russian Federation Who Have Finished Exercising Their Powers*[36] signed in May 2008. At present, it remains the only presidential center in the country, even though Yeltsin is not the only Russian leader whose presidency has ended. The law was created along the lines of the United States institutional commemoration of former executive leaders, which consists of the creation of presidential memorials, libraries, and multifunctional cultural centers. These sites are intended to shape public memory related to the country's political history and project a certain self-image of the nation – to be «[...] nodal points for the negotiation of who we are as a people and where we are going, politically and culturally»[37], as suggested by Benjamin Hufbauer.

Having failed to find a suitable plot of land within Yekaterinburg city center, Yeltsin's family accepted an offer to take over a construction site of the Demidov business and commercial complex designed by Sergey Aleinikov. In order to transform a 9-story congress hall into a new architectural body capable of transmitting the identity of a cultural institution and communicating with the existing urban context explicitly and innovatively, the Yeltsin Center's architect Boris Bernaskoni[38] designed a large-scale architectural scenery: an irregular frame structure extending across the façade of the already existing body. Connecting the rooftop of the building, the public *piazza* in front of the main entrance and the building's central cylindrical volume, the new element seeks to provide more aesthetic than functional solutions: entirely covered by three-layer perforated GRADAS steel panels that contain 2 500 sqm of video-capable LED-RGB pixels between the glass cladding and continuous external membrane, the frame structure becomes an exterior digital display. Dynamic digital content is broadcasted on its entire surface transforming it into a high-resolution media façade.

The range of the center's mandatory functions determined by the federal law included a presidential archive, a library, and a museum. Bernaskoni decided to extend it to transform an existing but uncompleted building into a cultural center with a highly multipronged program. Along with the museum, the center hosts exhibition spaces, conference venues, a presidential archive, a library, spaces for pedagogical activities for both adults and children, multiple offices, a restaurant, a bookshop, a co-working, a multifunctional and widely adaptable atrium (3 000 sqm at the ground floor level) featuring facilities and equipment for video projection, recreation, and public events. In addition to the spaces managed directly by the Yeltsin Centre, various floors of the atrium zone are occupied by numerous commercial facilities. The absence of clear spatial division between cultural and non-cultural facilities is one of the architectural project's serious flaws: it weakens the status of the presidential center as a major cultural institution.

For the Perm-36 Memorial Museum in the Perm region, the Sakharov Center in Moscow, the GULAG History State Museum in Moscow, and the Boris Yeltsin Museum in Yekaterinburg, a further critical and practical selection has been applied to adopt an in-depth approach. The critical criterion consists of selecting the museums featuring the most valuable museographic projects. As a result, four in-depth case studies were performed with the dual objective of highlighting the specific features of the Russian museological state of affairs in the realm of dissonant memories and of exploring the museum's role as a political instrument in post-Soviet Russia.

Museum and Exhibition Design as Political Instruments

The international museological practice of the previous three decades is considered by a great number of researchers as resulting in a self-contained phenomenon of architectural and exhibition design evolution – a phenomenon of the contemporary museum[1]. In an increasingly globalized sociocultural space, museums embody the most important trends of the postmodern cultural paradigm, as well as the development of technologies and highly interpretive methods of architectural design, construction, and museum display design.

The previous model of the modern museum, which in its turn follows on from the elitist, conservative, and taxonomic classical museum, has been and continues to be thoroughly studied by leading museologists of the day[2]. In modern Western practice, especially since World War II, museums should not only fulfill their traditional functions – storage of the collections and their public exhibition – but become a place for carrying out socially significant processes, such as the unification of various social groups under the aegis of diverse cultural and educational activities. A mandatory requirement for the modern museum complex is to find the most effective ways of influencing the visitor, and the first way of achieving this task is through architecture: architectural expression is committed to creating the immersive ambience for an artifact that has been removed from its original context. It thus gains a high level of social value. On the other hand, another key task of museum architecture is to «create the ambience for the public», using the terms of Italian

45

architect F. Albini: «It [architecture] creates a modern atmosphere around the visitor, and precisely because it is modern, it directly enters into the relationship with the visitor's sensitivity, with his culture, with his mentality of a modern man»[3].

A significant shift in the role of the museum in society between the 1980s and 1990s led to the formation of new methods of architectural and exhibition design. By assuming a wide range of tasks (sociocultural, educational, sociopolitical, commercial, role in the urban planning development, and many others), the museum seeks to organically combine the functions of exhibition space, an educational center, an archive, a media library, an office building for hundreds of museum professionals, a store, a restaurant, and a public forum. The contemporary museum endeavors to create the most effective translation of rich, complex, synthetic information by developing various design strategies.

The following trends can be traced in the architectural and interior solutions of museums of the contemporary period: a retreat from the already established methods of architectural planning; the embodiment of the ideas of plasticity and independent imagery of the museum environment; implementation of a qualitatively new high-tech level of exhibition design, where each exhibit interacts with its surrounding environment. Non-linear methods of architectural and interior design, often implying paradoxical solutions from the point of view of traditional planning, are due to the development of a new scientific picture of the world[4].

Concurrently, according to Luca Basso Peressut, the contemporary museum follows an inclusive strategy towards the experience of its past:

> Museum architecture at the dawn of the new millennium postulates the absorption of all previous experience in a *continuum* of reformulations that are constructed through the use of typological, formal, exhibitive fragments taken in conscious liberty from the classical tradition, as well as from that of the Modern Movement[5].

Many scholars also highlight that contemporary museums are complex and sometimes contradictory institutions engaged in the constant pursuit of novelty and attractiveness[6]. The core communication requirement for a contemporary museum consists of seeking the most powerful representational methods aimed at sensitizing and influencing the viewer. The processes of "sense-making" and "affect-making" within the museum institution involve the implementation of effective exhibition design strategies, which are potentially sustainable in the long term. These strategies, among others, include the development of diverse scenarios of interaction between the museum environment and the audience, generating potent – sometimes unexpected – emotional and sensory effects, applying up-to-date technologies, etc.

Concerning museums addressing dissonant memories, the choice of ways and means of influencing visitors stems from the political character of museum representations. As argued by professor Christopher

Whitehead, a leading scholar in the field of museology and critical heritage, the museum display is «[...] a political, public production of propositional knowledge intended to influence audiences and to create durable social effects»[7]. Within this perspective, narrative museum abstractions are materialized «[...] by configurations of material proofs set up in displays to renew conditions of *witnessing*, allowing for the reproduction of singular truth»[8]. This scientific standpoint is particularly crucial for understanding the cause-and-effect relationships behind certain strategies of exhibition design in Russian museums dealing with political history.

Architectural and exhibition design practice of the 1990s–2010s reflects the characteristic feature of the transitional era – a continuous search for the lost holistic, synthetic worldview, which stems from the radical breakdown of paradigms between the 1980s and 1990s. In the particular case of Russia, this breakdown was considerably reinforced by the dissolution of the Soviet Union. Starting from the 1990s, Russian architects were continuously and not always successfully trying to transfer the experience of contemporary Western architectural practice to the realities of the post-Soviet country[9]. Therefore, even if the Russian museum design practice of the last three decades has not reached the level of any Western country, it is entirely permissible to analyze this practice using the contextual framework of contemporary Western museology.

From the perspective of contemporary museum design, the cases of the GULAG History State Museum and the Boris Yeltsin Museum are of major interest. A synthesis of the unique architectural image and exhibition environment of these cases results in a complex functional and aesthetic understanding of a museum project. In the case of the Gulag History State Museum and the Sakharov Center, visual interpretation of a museum concept is provided through the design of a multipronged and mediative museum display based on a qualitatively new level of exhibition design in the context of early post-Soviet practice. Along with the Perm-36 Memorial Museum, these are examples of a strong bottom-up initiative in the field of memory culture throughout the 1990s and early 2000s.

The first permanent exhibition project *Political Repression in the USSR (1917–1991)* of the Perm-36 Memorial Museum was designed by the team of museum founder V. Shmyrov in 1995[10]. The first museum display included archival materials, photographs, and several artifacts. In 1998, the exhibition *Prisoners of the Special Regime Barracks* was opened in the main building of the special security zone. Since then the permanent exhibition has undergone multiple changes, and numerous temporary exhibition projects have been carried out by the museum staff. The exhibition *GULAG: History, Work, Life* inaugurated in 2003, constituted the core of the permanent museum display during the following decade.

In 2011–2012, the museum collaborated with Ralph Appelbaum Associates (RAA) to create a new comprehensive permanent exhibition. In 2012, the

Ralph Appelbaum Associates project was rejected by the then Perm region governor Victor Basargin. Paul Williams, who was directly involved in this project, claimed that – at the time – the Perm-36 Memorial Museum was looking forward to reaffirming its status as the memory site of primary importance:

> Perm-36 is looking to secure funding to develop within its buildings full, media-rich exhibition environments that will bring to life and add context to its original barracks. With a light-touch approach to the existing architecture – films, audio-visual projections, and multimedia digital environments are planned[11].

In 2018, Shmyrov declared that, after the change of administration in 2014, part of the existing exhibitions had been destroyed or closed[12], while the new director Natalya Semakova insisted that all valuable museum displays remaining from Shmyrov's team had been carefully preserved. However, the question of public access to these displays remains open: no free circulation is admitted on the museum's premises, and visitors can only enter the former camp if accompanied and guided by members of the museum staff, who open exhibition spaces to them.

In March 2018, when the author visited the museum, permanent (about a third of the floor area dedicated to the museum display) and temporary exhibitions extending over a total of 1 500 sqm were arranged in the headquarter building, habitable barrack, auditorium, workshops, and the special security barrack.

During the meeting with the author, Semakova declared she had tripled the museum's exhibition spaces since being appointed director. Indeed, some new exhibition spaces have been arranged inside the workshops by the new administration. But no official information about the floor area used for the museum display having been extended from 500 to 1 500 sqm could be found in official public sources. For instance, the annual performance report submitted by Semakova to senior authorities on January 11, 2019, states that «[...] the restoration and repair works amounting to 2 678 400 rubles [circa 33 700 euros] have been performed in 2018»[13]. However, no data about the aforementioned floor area extension is provided in the document.

The permanent exhibition *GULAG: History, Work, Life* is still located in one of the spaces of the wooden habitable barrack. The display illustrates the history of the USSR's forced labor camps starting with the first detention facilities of the 1920s. The original items owned by Gulag prisoners (about 30 items) are placed inside three prismatic display cases in the center of the 60 sqm room. The continuing display installation, similar to a system of barbed-wire fences, contains NKVD archival documents, photographs, and panels with texts. Despite a strong emotional sensation left by the entire composition and a high scientific value of the contents, the display shows limited communication capacity deriving from a weak design strategy: it features a great amount of highly complex information represented rather chaotically in a small space, as well as an awkward arrangement of artifacts (the display cases are too low, and some items inside them are almost at floor level). Furthermore, a system of spotlights has recently been replaced by fluorescent lamps, which make the exhibition lighting inappropriate.

Other interior spaces of the habitable barrack contain period rooms and small themed displays showing the everyday life of camp prisoners. Shmyrov's team managed to preserve the authentic austerity of such spaces as the convicts' personal belongings storage room, cloakroom, lavatory, dormitory, and the "red corner room"[14] by introducing original elements of the interior environment or high-quality replicas (for instance, wooden beds in the dormitory).

Concerning the exhibition projects carried out by the new museum administration, the most eloquent example is the 2016 display *National Memory Site* inaugurated inside the special security barrack after its protracted closure, reported via various sources[15]. The administration painted the interiors of the barrack making multiple inscriptions and graffiti on its walls. Shmyrov argued this to be a «barbarous» attitude to the contentious heritage site: «The cramped cells [...] are filled with exhibits temporarily brought here from other museums. They are rare and valuable but still alien to this place»[16]. The scientific framework of the display is inadequate in comparison to the exhibitions made by Shmyrov's team and to the importance of the site. Finally, within the contents of the display, no particular attention was paid to the fact that the barrack had been mostly occupied by Lithuanians, Estonians, and Ukrainians struggling for the liberation of their republics.

When the author visited the Perm-36 Memorial Museum in March 2018, the display had been partially removed. Yet several cells of the barrack were occupied by exhibition panels revealing the display's extremely low design quality. Some written content was printed on A4 sheets of paper and left on the floor, placed vertically against the wall. The corridor was once again repainted. One of the cells was completely draped in white tulle and illuminated with a dim light in order to create a space for recreation and reflection. The striking inappropriateness of this interior inside a Gulag special security cell bears witness to the level of incompetence of the museum's new administration.

The design concept of the Sakharov Center's permanent museum display, inaugurated in 1997, was created by internationally renowned Russian architect Eugene Asse[17]. However, the display became a result of multidimensional scientific, design, and manufacturing work carried out by a team of professionals including the members of Architectural Laboratory, a group of young architects founded by Asse in 1994, as well as the members of Iced Architects, a group founded in 1993 by architects I. Bilashenko and I. Voznesensky. Display contents were elaborated by M. Gnedovsky, N. Okhotin, L. Litinsky, and G. Averbukh, and subsequently updated in the early 2000s under the guidance of Y. Samodurov, L. Vasilovskaya, A. Ermolaev, A.

Ivanov, and M. Kudyukina. The exhibition equipment was developed, produced, and installed by the company Bioinjector. In 1997, the project was awarded the Moscow Architectural Competition prize in the category "Architecture and Design".

The exhibition located in the area of about 200 sqm on the first floor of the Sakharov Center presents the history of the USSR from 1917 to 1991, through the prism of political repression and public resistance to the Soviet regime. Asse suggested dividing the interior into four aisles to create a specific itinerary, developed following the narrational logic: three walls serving as exhibition stands partition the rectangular hall and transform it into a multifunctional museum space. The permanent exhibition is hosted in aisles A (*Mythology and Ideology in the USSR*, *Political Repression in the USSR*) and B (*Way through the Gulag*, *Resistance to Unfreedom in the USSR*), while the temporary exhibitions are arranged in aisle C using foldable modular stands made of steel and glass. Finally, aisle D hosts another permanent display (*Andrey Sakharov. Personality and Fate*) dedicated to Sakharov's life, his participation in the dissident movement, and his key political role in the process of the democratic formation of the opposition in the late 1980s.

Asse uses different materials for the side surfaces of each aisle in the following order: the original brickwork of the 19th-century museum building, metal, oriented strand board, and fabric. The intentional metaphor of rough and heavy materials followed by lighter, softer ones reflects the contextual concept of the museum's permanent exhibition: an ascension from misery, crime, and death to the individual's struggle for freedom represented by the personality of A. Sakharov, a struggle that is supposed to lead society to a brighter future.

The red brick wall of the first display representing contentious histories of the early Leninist-Stalinist period is a reference to the Kremlin walls, the primary semiotic representation of absolute political power and ideological monopoly in Russian culture. The metal wall facing it contains a selection of key archival documents and photographs, such as one of Stalin's many resolutions ordering the execution of 6 600 people. Thanks to a high level of scientific work and rigorous graphic articulation carried out by historians (for instance, by Nikita Okhotin, one of the leading Russian scholars in the field of Stalinism) and designers, nine panels with 196 documents hung on a metal wall give a clear and expressive image of Stalin's Great Terror, and at the same time avoid an excess of information, ambiguity, or sense of aloofness often generated by Soviet history exhibitions in today's Russia[18]. The design solution of the second aisle is similar to an artwork, a multilayered, multi-material installation containing artifacts, documents, and audiovisual elements. On the right-hand side (*Way through the Gulag*), the collective memory of mass repression is represented by personal items and photographs of Gulag prisoners, scattered pieces of wood, and NKVD files, which remain "imprisoned" behind the continuous metal grid. Here not only is the grid a visual and spatial framework organizing the display but a design leitmotif as well: it is reflected on the opposite side of the aisle (*Resistance to Unfreedom in the USSR*) in the form of wooden display cabinets containing exhibits and text panels in which Khrushchev's de-Stalinization and the history of the Soviet dissident movement are narrated. Political history is represented here through tangible and intangible elements of collective memory: objects of everyday life, books, images, as well as commonplace expressions and jokes of the time.

Critically speaking, the 23-year-old small-scale permanent exhibition of the Sakharov Center reveals its extremely limited non-governmental budget and an obvious lack of up-to-date technologies in museum communication. At the same time, it constitutes a rare example of how effectively Soviet dissonant memories and contentious histories can be represented in post-Soviet museum displays. Scientific authenticity, rigorous selection of exhibits, high-quality design implementation, and particular attention to intense emotional effects provide optimal results in terms of mediation between the display and the public. The vibrant, sensory exhibition environment of the Sakharov Center achieved by strong and sustainable design solutions continues to engage with the visitor's sensitivity and «[...] with his mentality of a modern man»[19].

On October 30, 2015, on the Day of Remembrance of the Victims of Political Repression, after eleven years of operation, the Gulag History State Museum inaugurated its new building granted by Moscow City

Government three years earlier, a 4-story Art Nouveau apartment building at 1st Samotechniy Lane built in 1906 by Russian architect Nikolay Ivanovich Zherikhov. The public competition for the declared "adaptive reuse" project was won by architectural firm PSU-5. At the same time, no detailed information about the competition can be found either on the firm's website[20] or in other public sources. Architect Dmitry Bariudin claims that the public competition was a mere formality:

> I am convinced that, under some kind of agreement about which I know nothing in particular, it had been clearly indicated that the PSU-5 firm had to do the design project. The outcome of the competition was known beforehand. [...] Making us enter into the project was quite difficult. A particular scheme allowing this to be done had been invented. In substance, we became the emissaries of the museum, which was criticizing the project of the PSU-5 and making modifications to it[21].

According to the officially approved project, the whole interior structure of the building had to be demolished due to its precarious state of conservation: the original exterior shell of the building was the only element left for an extensive recovery[22]. When the PSU-5 had already finished the demolition works and was constructing the new steel-framed structure inside the shell, museum director Roman Romanov invited Igor Aparin and Dmitry Bariudin, co-founders of the Kontora architectural bureau, to join the project. The decision to give *special status* to the architects Romanov already knew was subsequently approved by the supervising Moscow Department of Culture. The Kontora bureau *de facto* thus became the main author of the completed reconstruction project, despite never having formally participated in the public competition for the new Gulag History State Museum building.

Except for the issues related to limited funding, the architects declare they have never received recommendations or restrictions from the Moscow Department of Culture. Compromises made by the Kontora bureau with the state authorities were mainly related to the quality of materials and design implementation. The new Gulag History State Museum reveals an unusually high level of architectural design quality in comparison with other newly established Russian museums dedicated to dissonant memories and political history. It shows strong results not only in terms of formal museological performance but also in terms of specific architectural expressiveness that this type of institution should embody to achieve a broad array of museum communication tasks.

The first exhibition *National Memory of the GULAG* inaugurated in the new museum building in October 2015 gathered exhibits not only from the museum's collection but from twenty-five other history museums around the country. The spatial division into two contextual storylines – several "spaces of memory" presenting documents, artifacts, and video testimonies of the Gulag survivors at floor level, and the displays on the history of the Gulag system at the entresols – carried a symbolic significance:

> Ascent to the entresols and access to the balconies [...] suggest the necessity to "soar" over some historical processes in order to understand what has happened. Then we go down to earth and dive into the documents and other evidence of the time[23].

The core theme of the exhibition was that of survival, both physical and emotional, in the inhuman conditions of Gulag prisons and camps: the main double-height space had been occupied by twenty "barrack-like" display cases showing aspects of prisoners' everyday life. The exhibition also featured interactive, even ludic installations and audiovisual features, such as a soundtrack of prison doors closing and bars locking for the first "space of memory" displaying original cell doors from various Gulag prisons; or a huge wooden sliding puzzle, where visitors are supposed to slide pieces of the White Sea-Baltic Canal map and thus open underlying boxes with artifacts and photographs of the Gulag prisoners constructing the canal.

The Kontora bureau's exhibition design has aroused debates among specialists from various fields[24]. Russian art theorist and historian Gleb Napreenko criticized the project for its excessive stylization, aestheticization, and entertainment appeal that are incompatible with its topic:

> Boxes for backpacks made of unpainted metal, à la Gulag tools. Brick walls, which, according to the designers, should resemble the walls of the prison. But if you think about it, the very idea of creating the Gulag style is shocking. And all these museum technologies for engaging the

visitor, such as the White Sea-Baltic Canal sliding puzzle or the roller with the lists of executed people, are given precisely in this design spirit[25].

In December 2018, the museum presented its permanent exhibition *The GULAG in People's Lives and the National History* also designed by the Kontora bureau. The exhibition contents were developed under the supervision of prominent Russian historian, Galina Mikhailovna Ivanova. According to Bariudin, both projects should be seen as conceptual statements:

> The old and new exhibitions are fundamentally different. The first one was generally about the volume of the building. It was a sort of introduction: we introduced the space and specified two layers of the Gulag phenomenon within this space. [...] There are a lot of layers [in today's exhibition]. The first and most important layer which, in my opinion, did not work out, is a kind of "ouroboros", a serpent that devours itself. It is as if you are entering the body of a worm, and it is gradually pushing you out with its muscles. It was the original concept, from which this space originates[26].

The sophisticated exhibition itinerary is also developed across two levels of the space: associated by the designers with a circular "ouroboros", the itinerary starts and ends at the entresols. However, the previous spatial division into the two realms of cognition in accordance with the upper and lower levels has not been maintained in the new museum display: the entresols are now merely the segments of a non-linear itinerary, not a key means for the physical and conceptual structuring of the exhibition space.

The floor level is now occupied by the ascetic display scenery running all the way around with a rigid pattern of movement: descending from the first entresol area, which features the original prison doors (now distributed at random across space), the visitor enters the maze formed by continuous displays and small rooms for audiovisual projections and interactive installations. A great deal of emotionally intense multimedia content in a fairly narrow, obscure space evokes a strong box-like feeling, creating obstacles for appreciation and sensory perception.

Bariudin admits that the architectural space is now less present in the exhibition environment: «We built up everything that we had so meticulously opened»[27]. Still visible in the side rooms are the brick walls of the building that become an integral part of the display imagery: seen in relation to the other materials, such as rough plaster walls or the floor finish, the brick surfaces generate a vibrant, spectacular contrast and enrich the possibilities for conceptual and decorative display solutions.

The exhibition itinerary leads visitors towards the culmination point of the entire composition's dramaturgy: at the end of the maze, visitors enter the dark empty room with a high false lightwell in the center. The room features an immersive audio installation: visitors are supposed to sit on the benches and listen to the voices reading the endless list of Gulag victims' names and sentences. Similar in type to the meditative Reflection Hall of Milan's Shoah Memorial[28], it is one of the most powerful experiences of the entire museum display: the itinerary becomes a metaphorical *Via Crucis* that requires mental and emotional self-sacrifice, while its culmination point reaches the peak of affective sensitization and stimulates further reflection on the Gulag-related past.

The redimension of the conceptual approach towards a closer, more intimate scale of trauma representation – the scale of a single individual and his personal history – is a significant enhancement of the permanent exhibition in comparison to the previous display. At the same time, the design solutions implemented are not entirely suitable in fulfilling the fundamental task of museum communication: that of unleashing the full mediative potential of the exhibition's diverse contents.

The Boris Yeltsin Museum, a semantic core of the presidential center in Yekaterinburg, is situated on the first and second floors of the building's cylindrical volume. The permanent exhibition is created by Ralph Appelbaum Associates in collaboration with Russian film director, Pavel Lungin. The design project is a result of a collective work of interior, multimedia, and graphic designers in cooperation with historians, president's biographers, and members of Yeltsin's inner circle.

The introductive 3D-animated film on Russian history is produced by the Main Road Post visual effects studio based in Russia. According to the museum's vice director Lyudmila Telen, the idea of the film representing Yeltsin's presidency as the culmination of the national history, as well as other conceptual elements of the exhibition project, were personally suggested by Yeltsin's daughter Tatyana Yumasheva[29].

The *Labyrinth* display on the first floor is dedicated to pre-Yeltsin times: Soviet history is represented here in parallel with the history of Yeltsin's family. A seamless and dense environment featuring a large number of text, graphic, audiovisual materials, and artifacts is structured according to the timeline indicated on the floor of a single linear space. The issues of difficult and contentious histories (for instance, mass murders during the 1917–1922 Civil War) are integrated into the displays along with elements of official propaganda (Soviet posters and newspaper headlines) so that the visitor can perceive the multilayered structure of the exhibition plot and make individual conclusions based on the variety of historical facts. This paradigm of individual learning through an orchestrated multisensorial experience – at times verging on entertainment and leisure – and supported by a wide range of material artifacts, interactive interfaces, and multimedia productions, has been exploited by RAA in many of their exhibition design projects. A similar approach has been applied by RAA to the permanent exhibition for the 2012 Jewish Museum and Tolerance Center in Moscow featuring a continuing sequence of compelling multisensory experiences, from «[...] theatrical settings that tell the story of Russian Jewry through large-scale immersive films, cutting-edge interactive experiences, oral-history theaters»[30] to a full-scale T-34 WWII-era tank and a Soviet military aircraft.

Both RAA's Russian exhibition projects show a high-quality design layout bringing a perceptible sense of accessibility, as well as an emphasis on everyday-life objects: in the case of the Boris Yeltsin Museum, the focus is on the then-future president's personal belongings located in the display cases in the middle of the hall. The general historical narration is crisscrossed with one concerning individual and family memory. An affective lighting strategy, which is based on a strong interplay of light and shade obtained by the screens and spotlighting of exhibits, is also similar to that used by the RAA for the paradigmatic case study of the permanent exhibition design of the 1993 United States Holocaust Memorial Museum.

Another part of the Boris Yeltsin Museum's permanent display – *Seven Days That Changed Russia* – is distributed over seven halls on its second floor. Each "day" corresponds to one of the major historical events of Yeltsin's presidency: *We Are Waiting for Changes!* (late *perestroika* years); *August Coup d'État* (defense of the White House and the collapse of the USSR); *Unpopular Measures* (first democratic reforms and their consequences); *Birth of a Constitution* (political crisis in October 1993); *Vote or Lose* (the 1996 presidential campaign); *Presidential Marathon* (Yeltsin's health problems during his second term); *Farewell to the Kremlin* (Yeltsin's resignation in December 1999). The access to each "day" is from the central hall covered with a glass dome. The massive curved wall with a screen, as well as the bench with a life-size bronze statue of Yeltsin "watching" an introductive biographical slideshow side-by-side with the visitors, constitute a suggestive *mise en scene*: images of political glory and success, together with the collection of Yeltsin's state decorations exhibited right under the screen, are juxtaposed with a more approachable, human-scale, even intimate image. This eloquent ambivalence of the president's personality became the main narrative of the entire exhibition.

Several interactive period rooms successively alternate with halls featuring the broadest range of documents, artifacts, kinetic models, immersive multimedia installations, holographic projections, visual and audio effects. The exhibition is distinguished by constant unpredictability, a high degree of both physical and emotional engagement, and a fundamentally new level of accessibility, in both the literal and metaphorical sense. Not only physical barriers between visitors and exhibits are diminished or removed: various dissonant memories of the immediate post-Soviet years (from the shortage of basic goods to the storming of the Ostankino television center during the 1993 constitutional crisis) transmitted through the *Seven Days that Changed Russia* display are intended to become shared memories of the majority of the museum's audience: generations who witnessed the difficulties of the 1990s and their children's generations.

However, not all of these memories can resonate with the individual's emotional truth. The clearest example is *The Chechen Tragedy* display inside the narrow, corridor-like space of the *Vote or Lose* exhibition hall. Several display cases with artifacts are integrated into the irregular wall, which is covered with a patchwork

65

of fake bullet halls. A vivid, glossy surface is contrasted with the opposite wall featuring a chronological compilation of images that are meant to illustrate the first Chechen war. The apparent inadequacy of the design solution regarding the most painful event in the history of post-Soviet Russia, which compromised the principles of democracy, freedom, and sovereignty proclaimed by Yeltsin in the early 1990s, shows that RAA's universal exhibition design language cannot be applied to any contentious historical context without a thorough preliminary research[31] and a conscious commitment by the client (in this case, the museum board represented by Yeltsin's family) to unfold these memories as extensively as possible.

The final part of the exhibition itinerary is *The Hall of Freedom* – a panoramic interior space with five columns in front of a curved curtain wall. The columns represented as symbolic "pylons of freedom" support LCD flat-panel monitors. Each visitor can record a short video about freedom, which will be shown on the screens, together with similar videos made by celebrities – actors, writers, politicians, etc. An active participatory strategy is applied to intensify the perception of personal involvement in the museum narration. The representation of the "place identity"[32] is used here as a link between physical forms of space (architectural, exhibition, and urban space) and perception of the museological narratives. This segment of the exhibition itinerary is an attempt to see the panorama of the city from a new perspective, a perspective that seeks to comprehend different stages in the history of Yekaterinburg and to establish both visual and semantic interactions with it.

Back in 2006, Jutta Scherrer[33] was concerned about the increasing legal pressure on Russian NGOs, especially those operating in the field of dissonant memories and contentious past. At that time, the Russian political class was taking the first steps towards controlling the memory culture on a national level[34]: Saint George's Ribbon, which, since 2005, had been promoted by Russian pro-governmental movements as a universal symbol of remembrance of the Soviet victory in World War II, and was soon monopolized by Russian and pro-Russian nationalists all over the post-Soviet space[35], or the attempt to establish a unique state-drafted history textbook for public schools, are part of this process.

The influential role of museological narratives in the state-sponsored institutionalization of the past has been particularly highlighted by German scholars in the 1970s–1980s, notably by philosopher Hermann Lübbe[36]. Sharon Macdonald[37] develops these theoretical arguments: she claims that contemporary museums working with memory shift the focus towards the more subjective and experiential. By conveying well-calibrated "past-presencing" narratives[38], museums or memory sites are expected to produce a highly affective response:

> Material heritage, in forms such as museums or sites, as well as performances of intangible heritage, typically provides a temporally distinct experience, set apart from the everyday – even if the topic on display is everyday life. This

is the "condensed time" of heritage – time that is in effect marked as available for experience with some kind of depth or intensity [...]. The act of witnessing, via heritage, makes it part of our lived experience. So too does the sensory and bodily engagement of the heritage experience – the sounds and smells, and sometimes feel and tastes, as well as sights, involved[39].

The Perm-36 Memorial Museum is the most eloquent example of an affective response. Despite a long-term lack of financial and organizational support, which made the museum unable to carry out avant-garde exhibition design projects, and the subsequent legitimized confiscation of Shmyrov's NGO property in the interest of the state, the authentic materiality of this unique Russian site of trauma remains crucial for the reconstruction of a living Gulag-related cultural memory. It is, however, important to understand which political positions and policy goals are behind the museological narratives of the memory site so that the visitors can deal with it and reflect on their own memory process.

The Perm-36 Memorial Museum represented by Shmyrov and his team continues to be part of the International Coalition of Sites of Conscience. As stated on the ICSC website, «[...] the Coalition continues to work with the original founders of Perm-36, assisting them in enhancing and expanding their work, which is currently focused on the development of a website documenting gulags and sites of detention»[40]. Such Russian memory sites as the NKVD Remand Prison in Tomsk and the Memorial Complex at Mednoe[41] are also part of the coalition, while the Katyn Memorial Complex, another key site of Soviet political repression along with the Perm-36 camp, has never managed to join the ICSC. Its permanent museum display *Russia and Poland. The 20th Century. Pages of History*, which is a result of significant public funding[42], features a high-quality exhibition design project conveying deliberately distorted narratives of the Soviet invasion of Poland and mass murders carried out by the NKVD. It seems that the coalition is not interested in collaborating with the memory site that is actively used by Putin's administration to wage memory wars against its geopolitical opponents[43].

In the case of the Sakharov Center, which has so far avoided the wave of monopolization of the memory field triggered by the state but remains under pressure from the 2012 Russian "foreign agent" law[44], particular interest lies in the narrative conveyed through the interior and exhibition design. As suggested by Grigory Revzin, the key narrative here is that of the neutrality of the museum space, as it is «[...] not a place for a creative gesture, but a place for someone else's life»[45]. The author does not fully agree with Revzin's assessment regarding the neutrality of the museum environment but agrees with the assumption concerning the focus on the individualization of dissonant memories: Eugene Asse has constructed the museum scenario around the personal storylines of the witnesses, with a particular focus on individual and family memory. A

69

similar type of narrative can be seen at the memorial complexes of Nazran and Nalchik, even if the quality of design solutions and the degree of engagement with the visitor's sensitivity are considerably lower than those of the Sakharov Center.

The creation of the new GULAG History State Museum which, according to V. Dubina, takes on the characteristics of a «national Gulag museum»[46], is a manifestation of the trend towards the centralization of cultural and educational institutions, as well as of the state's entire ideological apparatus: it becomes a "sterile machine" for the production of controlled memories. However, the complexity of this case study lies in the ambiguity of its narratives.

On the one hand, the museum is directly involved in the creation of state policies regarding the memorialization of the victims of Soviet political repression[47]. On the other hand, the exclusion of the word "state" from all visual forms of representation of the museum in the public field (from the official website to the museum merchandise) can be seen as an attempt to disassociate itself from the image of a state-controlled institution. The previous permanent exhibition, inaugurated together with the new museum building in 2015, included a final video featuring Vladimir Putin, Moscow mayor Sergey Sobyanin and Patriarch Kirill: in their statements, they were explicitly supporting the memory policy represented through the museum narratives. The video was later removed, and the current permanent display mentions Sobyanin only in its end credits, together with other local officials. The architectural design of the museum was meant to «work on its collection» and «to create an environment for its perception»[48]. But instead, its «temple-like monumentality»[49] engenders an aesthetic appeal and a sense of awe in the audience. This is in line with today's Russian «park of culture», using the term by Mikhail Iampolski, where the state-sponsored memories become an assemblage of suggestive images appealing mostly to a sense of style and overshadowing issues of traumatic histories[50].

Finally, Romanov sees the new GULAG History State Museum as an institution that will help visitors «[...] to understand and accept what has happened»[51]. However, within the museum's system of "past-presencing" narratives, the idea of individualistic acceptance of trauma is transformed into the concept of an overall state-guided reconciliation that does not imply any other reaction. These narratives are an integral part of the contemporary Russian cultural and political landscape, where grassroots organizations such as the Memorial NGO or the Sakharov Center are declared "foreign agents", and the Perm-36 Memorial Museum founders are deprived of their private museum collection.

As in the case of the GULAG History State Museum, the Yeltsin Center's narrative apparatus has been politically instrumentalized to gain soft power control over an important cultural segment of one of the major Russian cities. The first and the only presidential center in post-Soviet Russia, it is seen by the Kremlin administration, whose actual high-level functionaries are members of its board[52], as an opportunity to generate the new image of an objectified state-approved historical truth. At the same time, according to such scholars as E. Boltunova, these goals have not been reached through architectural means or by the exhibition design. The attempt to adapt the initially poor architectural project lowers the status of a key public institution, and the museum exhibition shows «[...] its dependence on a political imaginary deeply rooted in Russian memorial practice that dates back to the imperial period and makes use of sacral (Russian Orthodox) and universalist interpretations of the images of past monarchs»[53].

The museum also appears to be a means of rhetorical influence for Yeltsin's family, which expects to remain part of the Russian political establishment. The idea of freedom, which constitutes the conceptual core of the whole museum project, is represented here "in Yeltsin's way" as the freedom granted to the people by the national leader.

The controversy of this narrative is highlighted by the architectural and exhibition design solutions: for instance, The Hall of Freedom, which is close in type to the recreation area of a prestigious shopping mall, does not seem to be suitable for its symbolical role. At the same time, the rhetorical representation of freedom, as understood by Yeltsin himself and his inner circle, is seen in the detailed reconstruction of the first president's office in the Kremlin: it conveys a strong sense of a liberal man in possession of monarchical power.

The present study is an exploration of a particular segment of contemporary Russian museum practice – that of selected museums addressing dissonant memories and political history – from perspectives of architectural, interior, and exhibition design, and in the light of the ongoing nationalization of historical memory started in 2012. During the last decade, Russian museums of political history are being exploited by the authorities for shaping an official, state-sponsored memory discourse concerning primarily the Soviet and immediate post-Soviet period.

The process of formation of fundamentally new cultural identities and, specifically, public policies in the field of memory is strongly apparent in today's Russia, which is shifting towards a more conservative, nationalist model in both foreign and domestic policies, and therefore progressively reviving neo-imperial rhetoric. In the case of museums dedicated to dissonant memories, contentious heritage, and the commemoration of traumatic histories, design practice is widely used as a political instrument of primary importance: it is an effective and efficient tool for transmitting specific messages that fit into the ideological framework of Putin's administration.

In his book *The Edifice Complex: How the Rich and Powerful Shape the World*, Deyan Sudjic analyses architecture as a manifestation of a self-glorifying political and economic power, a strategic means of mass communication, which is used to impose some sort of communal identity by the strength of architectural expressiveness and spectacularity:

> Above all, architecture is the means to tell a story about those who build it. [...] architecture is both a practical tool and an expressive language, capable of carrying highly specific messages. [...] There may be no fixed political meaning to a given architectural language, but that does not mean that architecture lacks the potential to assume a political aspect. Few successful architects can avoid producing buildings with a political dimension at some point in their career, whether they want to or not. And almost all political leaders find themselves using architects for political purposes[54].

In this perspective, museums dealing with political history appear to be of primary importance: endowed with iconic strength, which is essential in their activity of «management and proposal of truths»[55], museums contain key representative narratives implemented through architectural and exhibition design. That makes them, on the one hand, legitimate cultural-political actors with their specific agenda and, on the other hand, powerful agents in creating and reaffirming the image of the nation[56].

Concerning the case studies, a critical analysis performed in the course of the research leads to the following conclusion: the quality of a formal and conceptual museum project directly depends on a current top-down policy of dissonant memories "past presencing", to use the term of S. Macdonald[57].

Suffering from the effects of victimhood and aiming to transform difficult, traumatic histories into an instrument of propaganda, the Russian political class sees itself as a predominant *Kulturträger*[58] at a nationwide level.

The overall situation in the contemporary Russian museological field of political history can be described as a hybrid one. Individual and community-level public initiatives flourished in the 1990s and, with regard to dissonant memories, resulted in the creation of the Perm-36 Memorial Museum, the Gulag History State Museum, and other important institutions. However, since the early 2000s, Russian authorities are actively involved in establishing control over such projects: depending on the situation, the methods of control range from patronage and financial subsidies in exchange for loyalty (cases of the Yeltsin Center and the Gulag History State Museum) to law-based restrictions and complete takeover (case of the Perm-36 Memorial Museum).

As in the case of the Perm-36 Memorial Museum, authorities often transmit contentious messages that contradict individual or collective memory (for instance, family memory) and engage in the rhetoric of self-victimization projected in both past and present. In the absence of a new cultural model to offer the world, today's Russia broadcasts myths about the Soviet Union, which are personally supported by the president[59]. These contentious messages are potentially dangerous not only on the national level, where they are exacerbating the division within society and can catalyze a memory-related crisis of national identity, but on an international level as well: we can see that with the recent tensions between Russia and the European Union over the Soviet invasion of Poland in 1939[60], or upon the European Parliament resolution

75

on the proclamation of 23 August as European Day of Remembrance for Victims of Stalinism and Nazism[61].

Given what is known about the crimes of the Soviet regime (including mass political repression against non-Soviet citizens, military invasions in other countries, or annexation of their territories, etc.), the museum narrative is an effective means to fuel this mythology, at least for domestic consumption. At the level of individual and family memory, Russian people know about the crimes committed by the state on both a national and international scale: for instance, the author's own family preserves a memory about repressed Latvians and Germans, witnessed by the author's great-grandfathers in the 1930s and 1940s. Therefore, the state-sponsored memory policy, which was initially introduced by the authorities in the early 2010s, is cautious and strategically calculated. Using a wide range of strategies, including those of architectural and exhibition design, they present complex narratives concerning the Soviet and immediate post-Soviet history, which contain the following message: we have committed multiple crimes solely against our people, and these «local distortions»[62] cannot diminish the greatness and glory of our country.

The above-mentioned narratives constitute the foundations of Putin's current ideology, and in the years ahead, the state apparatus will continue to draw on cultural and educational resources, including those of museum development and communication, in order to obtain full nationalization of the history and memory discourse in the country. Critical analysis of architectural and exhibition design of Russian museums dedicated to political history, among other research studies, will help to identify and understand these ideological dynamics.

Notes

Multidimensional Memory: In Search of a Theoretical Framework

1. J. S. Eder, *Holocaust Angst: The Federal Republic of Germany and American Holocaust Memory since the 1970s*, Oxford University Press, Oxford and New York, 2016.

2. The so-called "historians' debate" (Germ. "Historikerstreit") started in 1986 when J. Habermas criticized the revisionist ideas of E. Nolte on the non-uniqueness and relative brutality of the Nazi crimes in comparison to other mass exterminations. Habermas characterized these ideas as "apologetic tendencies" (J. Habermas, 'A Kind of Settlement of Damages [Apologetic Tendencies]', trans. by J. Leaman, *New German Critique*, no. 44, 1988 [1986], pp. 25-39).

3. P. Nora, ed., *Les lieux de mémoire*, Gallimard, Paris, 1984–1992.

4. P. Nora, 'Between Memory and History: Les Lieux de Mémoire', trans. by M. Roudebush, *Representations*, no. 26, 1989, pp. 18-19.

5. The term "les non-lieux de la mémoire" appears for the first time in C. Lanzmann & F. Gantheret, 'The Non-Sites of Memory', *Nouvelle Revue de Psychanalyse*, vol. 33, 1986, p. 12.

6. M. Halbwachs, *On Collective Memory*, trans. and ed. by L. A. Coser, The University of Chicago Press, London and Chicago, 1992 [1950], p. 53.

7. P. Burke, 'History as Social Memory', in T. Butler, ed., *Memory: History, Culture, and the Mind*, Blackwell, Oxford, 1989, pp. 97-113.

8. J. K. Olick & J. Robbins, 'Social Memory Studies: From "Collective Memory" to the Historical Sociology of Mnemonic Practices', *Annual Review of Sociology*, vol. 24, 1998, pp. 105-140.

9. J. Assmann, *Das Kulturelle Gedächtnis: Schrift, Erinnerung und Politische Identität in frühen Hochkulturen*, C.H. Beck, Munich, 1992, pp. 52-53.

10. A. Assmann, *Zeit und Tradition: kulturelle Strategien der Dauer Duration*, Böhlau, Cologne, 1999, p. 64; J. Assmann, *Religion and*

Cultural Memory: Ten Studies, trans. by R. Livingstone, Stanford University Press, Stanford, 2006, pp. 8-9.

11. A. Assmann, *Erinnerungsräume: Formen und Wandlungen des kulturellen Gedächtnisses*, 2nd ed., C.H. Beck, Munich, 2003 [1999], p. 15.

12. A. Assmann, 'Response to Peter Novick', *Bulletin of the German Historical Institute*, no. 40, 2007, pp. 37-38.

13. A. Assmann, *Das neue Unbehagen an der Erinnerungskultur: Eine Intervention*, C.H. Beck, Munich, 2013; A. Assmann, *Shadows of Trauma: Memory and the Politics of Postwar Identity*, trans. by S. Clift, Fordham University Press, New York, 2016.

14. C. De Cesari & A. Rigney, 'Introduction', in C. De Cesari & A. Rigney, eds, *Transnational Memory: Circulation, Articulation, Scales*, De Gruyter, Berlin, 2014, pp. 1-25.

15. M. Hirsch, *Family Frames: Photography, Narrative, and Postmemory*, Harvard University Press, Cambridge, 1997, p. 22.

16. M. Hirsch, *The Generation of Postmemory: Writing and Visual Culture After the Holocaust*, Columbia University Press, New York, 2012.

17. A. Assmann, 2016, op. cit.

18. ibid., p. 239.

19. M. Iampolski (*Park Kultury: Kultura i nasilie v Moskve segodnya*, Novoe Izdatelstvo, Moscow, 2018, pp. 130-131) argues the role of rampant affects in contemporary Russian society and their impact on the socio-cultural environment. Issues related to Russian "postmemory" (or, more precisely, "postcatastrophic memory") are addressed in A. Etkind, *Warped Mourning: Stories of the Undead in the Land of the Unburied*, Stanford University Press, Stanford, 2013.

20. R. Sendyka ('The Difficult Heritage of Non-Sites of Memory: Contested Places, Contaminated Landscapes', *TRACES Journal,* vol. 3, 2017, pp. 4-15) cites a broad range of related works, such as a photographic series by D. Reinarz and C. Graf von Krockow (*Deathly Still: Pictures of Former Concentration Camps*, trans. by I. Flett, Scalo, New York, 1995), a publication by A. Huyssen ('The Voids of Berlin', *Critical Inquiry*, vol. 24, no. 1, 1997, pp. 57-81), a novel by J. S. Foer (*Everything Is Illuminated*, Houghton Mifflin, New York, 2002) and a reportage by M. Pollack (*Kontaminierte Landschaften: Unruhe bewahren*, Residenz Verlag, St. Pölten, 2014).

21. M. Tumarkin, *Traumascapes: The Power and Fate of Places*

Transformed by Tragedy, Melbourne University Press, Melbourne, 2005.

22. M. Nuttall, 'Memoryscape: A Sense of Locality in Northwest Greenland', *North Atlantic Studies*, vol. 1, no. 2, 1991, pp. 39-50.

23. M.-C. Garden, 'The Heritagescape: Looking at Landscapes of the Past', *International Journal of Heritage Studies*, vol. 12, no. 5, 2006, pp. 394-411.

24. M. Pollack, 2014, op. cit.

25. P. Violi, 'Trauma Site Museums and Politics of Memory', *Theory, Culture & Society*, vol. 29, no. 1, 2012, p. 39.

26. R. van der Laarse, 'Beyond Auschwitz? Europe's Terrorscapes in the Age of Postmemory', in M. Silberman & F. Vatan, eds, *Memory and Postwar Memorials: Confronting the Violence of the Past*, Palgrave Macmillan, New York, 2013, pp. 71-92.

27. R. van der Laarse, F. Mazzucchelli & C. Reijnen, 'Introduction: Traces of Terror, Signs of Trauma', in R. van der Laarse, F. Mazzucchelli & C. Reijnen, eds, *'Traces of Terror, Signs of Trauma': Practices of (Re)Presentation of Collective Memories in Space in Contemporary Europe (VS Versus, no. 119)*, Bompiani, Milano, 2014, pp. 3-19.

28. S. Macdonald, 'Theorizing Museums: An Introduction', in S. Macdonald & G. Fyfe, eds, *Theorizing Museums: Representing Identity and Diversity in a Changing World*, Blackwell, Oxford, 1996, p. 3.

29. S. Macdonald, 'Unsettling Memories: Intervention and Controversy over Difficult Public Heritage', in M. Anicio, & E. Peralta, eds, *Heritage and Identity. Engagement and Demission in the Contemporary World*, Routledge, London and New York, 2008, pp. 93-104; S. Macdonald, *Difficult Heritage: Negotiating the Nazi Past in Nuremberg and Beyond*, Routledge, London and New York, 2009.

30. ibid., p. 1.

31. T. Bennett, *The Birth of the Museum: History, Theory, Politics*, Routledge, London and New York, 1995, p. 63.

32. S. Macdonald, 1996, op. cit., p. 14.

33. A detailed research on how this potential is harvested within the contemporary museum practice on both national and international levels has been provided in course of the 2016–2019 *TRACES* research project led by L. Basso Peressut and F. Lanz, as well as in P. Williams, *Memorial Museums: The Global Rush to Commemorate Atrocities*, Berg, Oxford and New York, 2007; E. Lehrer, C. E. Milton & M. E. Patterson, eds, *Curating Difficult Knowledge: Violent Pasts* *in Public Places*, Palgrave Macmillan, New York, 2011; P. Williams, 'The Memorial Museum Identity Complex: Victimhood, Culpability, and Responsibility', in B. M. Carbonell, ed., *Museum Studies: An Anthology of Contexts*, Blackwell, Oxford, 2012, pp. 97-115; C. Whitehead et al., eds, *'Placing' Europe in the Museum: People(s), Places, Identities*, Politecnico di Milano, Milan, 2013; J. Rose, *Interpreting Difficult History at Museums and Historic Sites*, Rowman & Littlefield, Lanham, 2016.

34. S. Macdonald highlights the difference between "musealization" and "museumification": while the first one is seen as a compensating «[...] form of temporal anchoring in the face of loss of tradition and unsettlement brought about by the increased tempo of technological and related change» (S. Macdonald, *Memorylands: Heritage and Identity in Europe Today*, Routledge, London and New York, 2013, p. 138), the second one becomes a postmodern simulation of the real.

35. J. E. Tunbridge & G. J. Ashworth, *Dissonant Heritage: The Management of the Past as a Resource in Conflict*, John Wiley & Sons, Chichester, 1995.

36. ibid., p. 30.

37. See, for instance, D. Khapaeva, 'Historical Memory in Post-Soviet Gothic Society', *Social Research*, vol. 76, no. 1, 2009, pp. 359-394; N. Koposov, *Memory Laws, Memory Wars: The Politics of the Past in Europe and Russia*, Cambridge University Press, Cambridge, 2017; M. Iampolski, 2018, op. cit.

38. S. Macdonald, 2008, op. cit.

39. A. Cento Bull & H. L. Hansen, 'On Agonistic Memory', *Memory Studies*, vol. 9, no. 4, 2015, pp. 390-404.

40. R. van der Laarse, ''They Did It to Us': Museography of Concurrent Memories After 1989', in D. Bechtel & L. Jurgenson, eds, *Museography of Violence in Central Europe and Ex-USSR*, Editions Kimé, Paris, 2016, pp. 213-232.

41. T. Sindbæk Andersen & B. Törnquist-Plewa, 'Introduction: Disputed Memories in Central, Eastern and South-Eastern Europe', in T. Sindbæk Andersen & B. Törnquist-Plewa, eds, *Disputed Memory: Emotions and Memory Politics in Central, Eastern and South-Eastern Europe*, De Gruyter, Berlin, 2016, pp. 1-17.

42. The term "remediation" is used here regarding cultural memory studies, referring to A. Erll & A. Rigney, 'Introduction: Cultural Memory and its Dynamics', in A. Erll & A. Rigney, eds, *Mediation, Remediation, and the Dynamics of Cultural Memory*, Walter de Gruyter, Berlin and

New York, 2009, pp. 4-9.

43. See, for instance, A. Etkind, 2013, op. cit.; D. Dondurei cited in I. Chechel, 'Daniil Dondurei: 'Sverhtsennosti' opiat' ostanavlivaiyt Rossiyu? Rossiiskaya gosudarstvennost': k etiologii sverhtsennostei', Gefter [website], 2 February 2015; N. Koposov, 2017, op. cit.

44. 'National Implementation of Agenda 21: Russian Federation', United Nations [website], December 1996.

45. Article 14 of the Constitution defines Russia as a secular state (*Konstitutsiia Rossiiskoi Federatsii: Ofitsialnoe izdanie*, Yuridicheskaya Literatura, Moscow, 2005 [1993], p. 8). At the same time, Federal Law no. 125-FZ specifically names Christianity, Islam, Buddhism, and Judaism among the religions that constitute part of the Russian historical heritage (Federal Law no. 125-FZ, *Sobraniye Zakonodatelstva RF*, no. 39/4465, 26 September 1997).

46. E.g., A. Etkind, *Internal Colonization: Russia's Imperial Experience*, Polity Press, Cambridge and Malden, 2011.

47. K. Parthé, 'Russia's "Unreal Estate": Cognitive Mapping and National Identity', *Kennan Institute Occasional Papers*, vol. 267, 1997, p. 2.

48. D. Dondurei cited in I. Chechel, 2015, op. cit.

49. Differentiation between various categories of social memory has been summarized in J. K. Olick, *The Politics of Regret: On Collective Memory and Historical* Responsibility, Routledge, London and New York, 2007, p. 92.

50. N. Koposov, 2017, op. cit.

51. The cult of the World War II victory through the major role of the Soviet Union under Stalin's rule has been particularly emphasized during the celebration of its 60th anniversary. Official delegations from 28 countries have participated in the Victory Day parade on Red Square on May 9, 2005. In 2021, only one foreign leader, Emomali Rahmon, has participated in the celebration.

52. D. Khapaeva, 2009, op. cit., p. 368.

53. N. Svanidze, 'Hard Day's Night: Nikolai Svanidze' [video recording], interviewed by A. Zhelnov et al., TV Rain [website], 4 May 2017, 18:20-18:50.

54. E.g., R. Menon & E. Rumer, *Conflict in Ukraine: The Unwinding of the Post-Cold War Order*, The MIT Press, Cambridge and London, 2015.

55. *International Historical Educational Charitable and Human Rights*

Society Memorial (also: *International Memorial*) is the oldest Russian NGO dealing with civil rights and history of the Soviet political repression. See M. Mikaelyan, *Dissonant Memories in the Post-Soviet Space: Newly Established Museums and Political History in Russia (1991–2016), Appendixes*, PhD diss., Politecnico di Milano, Milan, 2020, pp. 16-23.

56. On the topic of Stalin's Great Terror, the author suggests to consult R. Conquest, *The Great Terror: A Reassessment*, Pimlico, London, 2008 [1968]; G. M. Ivanova, *Istoriya GULAGa, 1918–1958: sotsialno-ekonomicheskiy i politiko-pravovoy aspekty*, Nauka, Moscow, 2006; L. Viola, *The Unknown Gulag: The Lost World of Stalin's Special Settlements*, Oxford University Press, Oxford and New York, 2009.

57. 'Stalinskie repressii: prestuplenie ili nakazanie?', VCIOM [website], 5 July 2017.

58. 'Politicheskiye presledovaniya 30–40 gg. XX veka: motivy i maschtaby', VCIOM [website], 2 October 2017.

59. R. Koselleck, 'Forms and Traditions of Negative Memory', in V. Knigge & N. Frei, eds, *Remembering Crimes: Dealing with the Holocaust and Genocide*, C.H. Beck, Munich, 2002, pp. 21-32.

60. The premiere of the *Nureyev* ballet staged by one of Russia's leading theater directors K. Serebrennikov had to take place in July 2017, but was canceled due to controversy over a number of scenes considered by authorities as illegal public propaganda of homosexuality. In June 2020, Serebrennikov was found guilty of embezzlement.

61. M. Iampolski, 2018, op. cit., p. 173.

62. On February 23, 2012, immediately after his re-election, Putin addressed the public with a highly patriotic speech. He ended it with the proclamation: «The battle for Russia continues, the victory will be ours!» ('Vystuplenie Vladimira Putina na mitinge v Luzhnikah', RIA Novosti [website], 23 February 2012), without specifying the enemy to fight against.

63. M. Iampolski, 2018, op. cit., pp. 173-174.

Post-Soviet Memories and Conflicts: A Multilayer Museum Mapping

1. M. Mikaelyan, 2020, op. cit., p. 54.

2. ibid., p. 55.

3. ibid., pp. 39-53.

4. To give an example of such a typology, the Bunker-42 Cold War Museum in Moscow can be mentioned. Arranged inside an underground former military site in the city center, it is an entertainment-oriented business facility, which offers its visitors the possibility «[...] to organize leisure activities for every taste», as stated on its official website (http://bunker42.com/eng/). Such museums are not part of the author's research framework.

5. G. Revzin, *Russkaya arkhitektura rubezha XX–XXI vv.*, Novoye Izdatelstvo, Moscow, 2013, p. 453.

6. I. Gololobov, 'The Soviet People: The Rise and Fall of an Ideological Federalism', in E. Kavalski & M. Zolkos, eds, *Defunct Federalisms: Critical Perspectives on Federal Failure*, Ashgate Publishing, Farnham and Burlington, 2008, p. 156.

7. The first Russian museum, Peter the Great's Kunstkamera (from Ger. *Kunstkammer* meaning "cabinet of curiosities"), was founded in 1714 in Saint Petersburg and opened to the public in 1719. On the topic of the first Russian public museums see, for instance, M. T. Maistrovskaya, *Muzey kak obyekt kultury: iskusstvo ekspozitsionnogo ansamblya*, Progress-Tradiziya, Moscow, 2015, pp. 204-229.

8. The first to claim this concept was Russian philosopher P. Y. Chaadaev: «However, situated between the two great divisions of the world, between East and West, with one elbow leaning on China and another on Germany, we should have [...] incorporated the history of the entire world into our civilization» (P. Y. Chaadaev, *Polnoe sobranie sochineniy i izbrannye pis'ma*, vol. 1, Nauka, Moscow, 1991 [1829], p. 329).

9. According to official statistical reports, the number of museums administrated by the Ministry of Culture of the Russian Federation increased from 2 047 to 2 758 in the period between 2000 and 2015 (*Rossiya v tsifrakh 2017: kratkiy statisticheskiy sbornik*, Federal State Statistics Service, Moscow, 2017, p. 160).

10. M. E. Kaulen, *Muzeyefikatsiya istoriko-kulturnogo naslediya Rossii*, Eterna, Moscow, 2012.

11. See the interview with V. Shmyrov (M. Mikaelyan, 2020, op. cit., pp. 24-32) describing the takeover of the Perm-36 Memorial Museum by the regional authorities.

12. P. Williams, 2012, op. cit.

13. Such famous Soviet dissidents as Sergei Kovalev, Vladimir Bukovsky, Valeriy Marchenko, Vasyl Stus (died in the solitary cell of the camp in 1985) were among them.

14. «Prisoners were kept in cramped cells that were unlocked only once a day so that they could walk around in a tiny exercise block. [...] If a prisoner did not complete his work plan, he was put into solitary confinement and on an even more meagre diet» (V. Shmyrov, 'The Gulag Museum', *Museum International*, vol. 53, no. 1, 2001, p. 26).

15. P. Williams, 'Treading Difficult Ground: The Effort to Establish Russia's First National Gulag Museum', in D. Poulot, J. M. Lanzarote Guiral & F. Bodenstein, eds, *National Museums and the Negotiation of Difficult Pasts [EuNaMus Report, no. 8]*, Linköping University Electronic Press, Linköping, 2012, pp. 111-121.

16. E. Abzalova, 'El Centro Conmemorativo de la Historia de la Represión Política "Perm-36"', in M. Alonso, ed., *El Lugar de la Memoria: La Huella del Mal Como Pedagogía Democrática,* Bakeaz, Bilbao, 2012, pp. 80-81.

17. V. Shmyrov, 2001, op. cit.

18. The term "museo diffuso", which refers to a museum institution as a network of historical buildings capable of creating a historical and cultural narrative within the framework of its territory, has been coined by Italian architect F. Drugman ('Il museo diffuso', *Hinterland*, no. 21-22, 1982, pp. 24-25).

19. Abbreviation OGPU-NKVD stands for Unified State Political Directorate – People's Commissariat of Internal Affairs. OGPU (NKVD from 1934), the state-security organization established by F. Dzerzhinsky, is responsible for carrying out mass repression in the USSR.

20. For a deeper knowledge of Sakharov's significance as a scientist and a public figure, see G. Gorelik & A. W. Bouis, *The World of Andrei Sakharov: A Russian Physicist's Path to Freedom*, Oxford University Press, Oxford and New York, 2005.

21. "Adaptive reuse", also termed as "remodelling", "rehabilitation", or "conversion", is the process of substantial altering of architecture, in which «[t]he function is the most obvious change, but other alterations may be made to the building itself such as the circulation route, the orientation, the relationship between spaces; additions may be built and other areas may be demolished» (G. Brooker & S. Stone, *Re-readings: Interior Architecture and the Design Principles of Remodelling Existing Buildings*, RIBA Enterprises, London, 2004, p. 11).

22. For more details on the 1990s–2000s Russian practice in the realm of architectural heritage, see D. Paramonova who explicitly denounced the years of rule of the Moscow mayor Yuri Luzhkov: «The principle "the new is better than the old" and "antique" stylization were equally revered by both the city administration and the citizens. [...] A unique combination of the administrative dictatorship of the previous era with new "commercial" priorities allowed a radical modification of Moscow at the whim of a single individual» (D. Paramonova, *Griby, mutanty i drugiye: arkhitektura ery Luzhkova*, Strelka Press, Moscow, 2013, p. 6).

23. The exact number of 493 269 deported Chechen-Ingush people can be found in the report of NKVD major general V. M. Bochkov to L. P. Beria from March 21, 1944 (in N. L. Pobol & P. M. Polyan, *Stalinskie deportatsii: 1928–1953*, MFD/Materik, Moscow, 2005, p. 467).

24. On the topic of the Katyn massacre, see W. Materski, A. M. Cienciala & N. S. Lebedeva, eds, *Katyn: A Crime Without Punishment*, Yale University Press, New Haven and London, 2007; A. E. Gurianov, A. Raczynski & A. Zenkevich, *Killed in Katyn: The Book of Memory of Polish Prisoners of War of the Kozelsk NKVD Camp Executed on 5 March 1940 by the Decision of the CPSU Central Committee Politburo*, Memorial NGO/Zvenya, Moscow, 2015.

25. ibid., p. 62.

26. *Agreement between the Government of the Russian Federation and the Government of the Republic of Poland on burial places and places of memory of heroes of war and repression* was signed on February 22, 1994.

27. According to T. Sniegon, the anti-liberal turn of Putin's third presidential term has set off a «war of memories» between Poland and Russia: «The reformatted Katyn memorial reflects the new trend of "patriotization" and de-traumatization of Soviet crimes. The national traumas are politically "instrumentalized", while killings and human rights violations are trivialized and marginalized» (T. Sniegon, 'A Transformation of the Memorial Site in Katyn', PONARS Eurasia [website], 14 June 2019).

28. From its opening in 2004, the institution was known under the name of GULAG History State Museum. Since 2018, the museum is publicly using a shorter version of its official name: the word "state" has been excluded from the website, the entrance sign, and from all newly printed materials.

29. G. Revzin, 'Repressii v naturalnuyu velichinu: Muzey istorii GULAGa', *Kommersant Weekend*, no. 30, 2009, p. 16.

30. M. Yurshina, 'Roman Romanov, Director of the GULAG History Museum: 'Most of All Repressed People Need Public Recognition'', Istoricheskaya pamyat': XX vek [website], 1 January 2013.

31. The new museum building provides 3 367 sqm of interior space versus 850 sqm of the previous one (Architectural Council of Moscow, 'Architectural Project for the Gulag Museum', Architectural Council of Moscow [website], 10 June 2015).

32. The exact number of 37 713 deported Balkars (37 103 people, as stated in the NKVD documents) can be found in H.-M. A. Sabanchiev, *Byli soslany navechno: Deportatsiya i reabilitatsiya balkarskogo naroda*, Elbrus, Nalchik, 2004, p. 17.

33. P. M. Polyan, *Istoriomor, ili trepanatsiya pamyati: Bitvy za pravdu o GULAGe, deportatsiyakh, voyne i Kholokoste*, AST, Moscow, 2016, p. 87.

34. In the 1930s–1950s, a system of 17 labour camp units situated across the region's territory became the basis of its economic development: the detainees were extensively involved in the mining complex, logging industry and transport construction.

35. A.-G. Tamvelius (1907–1959) was born in Estonia. He was arrested in 1944 on charges of espionage and sentenced to 20 years of imprisonment. Tamvelius was released in 1956. In 1991, the Russian Federation exonerated him of all charges.

36. Federal Law no. 68-FZ, *Sobraniye Zakonodatelstva RF*, no. 20/2253, 13 May 2008.

37. B. Hufbauer, *Presidential Temples: How Memorials and Libraries Shape Public Memory*, University Press of Kansas, Lawrence, 2005, p. 7.

38. B. Bernaskoni is a graduate of the Moscow Architectural Institute. In 2008, his project of the PERMMUSEUM, the museum of contemporary art in the city of Perm, won an international competition presided over by P. Zumthor, leaving Zaha Hadid Architects and more than 300 other bureaus behind. The choice to invite B. Bernaskoni to work on the architectural design of the center came from the Yeltsin's family.

Museum and Exhibition Design as Political Instruments

1. See, for instance, A. Witcomb, *Re-Imagining the Museum: Beyond the Mausoleum*, Routledge, London and New York, 2003; K. Message, *New Museums and the Making of Culture*, Berg, Oxford and New York, 2006; S. Macleod, L. Hourston Hanks & J. Hale, eds, *Museum Making: Narratives, Architectures, Exhibitions*, Routledge, London and New York, 2012; K. Tzortzi, *Museum Space: Where Architecture Meets Museology*, Routledge, London and New York, 2015.

2. E.g., M. D. Levin, *The Modern Museum: Temple or Showroom*, Dvir Publishing House, Tel Aviv, 1983; T. Bennett, 1995, op. cit.

3. F. Albini cited in L. Basso Peressut, *Il Museo Moderno: Architettura e museografia da Auguste Perret a Louis I. Kahn*, Edizioni Lybra Immagine, Milan, 2005, p. 221.

4. I. A. Dobritsina, *Ot postmodernizma – k nelineynoy arkhitekture. Arkhitektura v kontekste sovremennoy filosofii*, Progress-Tradiziya, Moscow, 2004.

5. L. Basso Peressut, 2005, op. cit., p. 12.

6. E.g., K. Message, 2006, op. cit.

7. C. Whitehead, 'Critical Analysis Tool (CAT): Why Analyze Museum Display?', Digital Cultures in Culture Lab, Newcastle University [website], 2016, p. 2.

8. ibid., p. 6.

9. G. Revzin, 2013, op. cit.

10. *Memorialnyy muzey istorii politicheskikh repressiy i totalitarizma. Kuchino (Permskaya oblast'). Otchot 1994/1995*, Memorial NGO Perm Branch/Perm Region Administration/Sotzium, Perm, 1996, p. 11.

11. P. Williams, 2012, op. cit., p. 116.

12. V. Shmyrov cited in M. Mikaelyan, 2020, op. cit., p. 28.

13. 'Otchet o vypolnenii gosudarstvennogo zadaniya no. 466 na 2018 god', Perm-36 Memorial Museum-Reserve of the History of Political Repression [website], 11 January 2019, p. 23.

14. "Red corner room" was a common space for political education and propaganda needs.

15. E.g., M. Gessen, 'How Arseny Roginsky Confronted the Politics of Memory in Russia', The New Yorker [website], 19 December 2017.

16. V. Shmyrov, ''Perm-36'. Reabilitatsiya repressiy', Memorial NGO Perm Regional Branch [website], 2016.

17. Doctor of Architecture, member of the European Cultural Parliament, winner of multiple architectural awards, participant of the Venice Architecture Biennale since 1995 and Commissioner of the Russian Pavilion between 2004 and 2006, E. Asse is also dean of the *MARCH* Architecture School in Moscow.

18. For instance, by the displays addressing issues of contentious Soviet past in the state-sponsored Historical Parks *Russia – My History*, which are spread across the country (see Z. Bogumil, *Gulag Memories: The Rediscovery and Commemoration of Russia's Repressive Past*, trans. by P. Palmer, Berghahn Books, Oxford and New York, 2018, pp. 197, 203-204).

19. F. Albini cited in L. Basso Peressut, 2005, op. cit., p. 221.

20. The project *17.0513-PZ Reconstruction of a Non-Residential Building to Accommodate the Gulag History State Museum* is mentioned on the PSU-5 website (https://psu-5.ru/nashi-raboty/proektirovanie/#). However, the author was not able to find any further official information about the public competition and the winning project.

21. D. Bariudin cited in M. Mikaelyan, 2020, op. cit., p. 33.

22. Hereinafter the author refers to data retrieved during the interview with D. Bariudin (ibid., pp. 33-38).

23. R. Romanov cited in Architectural Council of Moscow, 2015, op. cit.

24. See, for instance, a critical analysis of the exhibition in V. Dubina, 'Virtualnoye mesto pamyati i realnoye prostranstvo GULAGa v sovremennoy Rossii', in A. Zavadsky, V. Sklez & K. Suverina, eds, *Politika affekta: muzej kak prostranstvo publichnoj istorii, Novoye literaturnoe obozrenie*, Moscow, 2019, pp. 329-331.

25. A. Vlasik, M. Yesipchuk & G. Naprenenko, 'Chto ne tak s novym Muzeyem istorii GULAGa', Colta.ru [website], 7 November 2016.

26. D. Bariudin cited in M. Mikaelyan, 2020, op. cit., pp. 35-36.

27. ibid.

28. The Shoah Memorial designed by Morpurgo de Curtis Architects is located in the spaces of Milan's Central Station used for the deportations of Jews and political convicts to the concentration camps during World War II.

29. I. Zhegulev, ''Ya schital sebya otvetstvennym za Putina'. Peryemnika Yeltsina privela k vlasti 'sem'ya', Meduza [website], 11 March 2019.

30. 'Jewish Museum and Tolerance Center', Ralph Appelbaum Associates [website], 2019.

31. The author assumes that this multidimensional research should be carried out across various fields of design, museography, semiotics, mnemonic studies, etc.

32. The notion of "place identity" has been developed by H. M. Proshansky, A. K. Fabian and R. Kaminoff as «[...] a sub-structure of the self-identity of the person consisting of, broadly conceived, cognitions about the physical world in which the individual lives» (H. M. Proshansky, A. K. Fabian & R. Kaminoff, 'Place-identity: Physical World Socialization of the Self', *Journal of Environmental Psychology*, vol. 3, no. 1, 1983, p. 59).

33. J. Scherrer, 'Russlands neue-alte Erinnerungsorte', *Aus Politik und Zeitgeschichte*, no. 11, 2006, pp. 24-28.

34. See, for instance, A. Miller & M. Lipman, eds, *Istoricheskaya politika v XXI veke*, Novoye literaturnoe obozrenie, Moscow, 2012.

35. The ribbon was originally part of the Order of Saint George, the highest military decoration for valour in the Russian Empire and, since 2000, in Russian Federation. M. Iampolski (2018, op. cit., p. 61) argues that the case of Saint George's Ribbon can be seen not only as an appropriation of collective memory but also as a fetishization of connective structures, to use the term coined by J. Assmann (1992, op. cit., p. 16).

36. H. Lübbe, *Der Fortschritt und das Museum. Über den Grund unseres Vergnügens an historischen Gegenständen*, Institute of Germanic Studies, London, 1982.

37. S. Macdonald, 2013, op. cit.

38. The term "past presencing" is introduced by S. Macdonald concerning «[...] the ways in which people variously draw on, experience, negotiate, reconstruct, and perform the past in their ongoing lives» (S. Macdonald, 'Presencing Europe's Pasts', in U. Kockel, M. N. Craith & J. Frykman, eds, *A Companion to the Anthropology of Europe*, Wiley-Blackwell, Chichester, 2012, p. 234).

39. S. Macdonald, 2013, op. cit., pp. 234-235.

40. 'Gulag Museum at Perm-36 (Russia)', International Coalition of Sites of Conscience [website], 2019.

41. The Memorial Complex at Mednoe is the site of mass murder of the Ostashkov camp prisoners.

42. According to the website of the Ministry of Culture of the Russian Federation, only in 2016–2017 the complex has received 126 mln rubles (circa 1,83 mln euros) of public funds ('Memorialnyy kompleks Katyn' budet dostroyen', Ministry of Culture of the Russian Federation [website], 7 August 2017).

43. For a comprehensive analysis of competing memories concerning the Katyn massacre, see A. Etkind et al., *Remembering Katyn*, Polity Press, Cambridge and Malden, 2012.

44. In 2014, the Russian Ministry of Justice declared the Sakharov Center to be a "foreign agent". The center was subsequently fined 300 000 rubles (4 700 euros) «[...] for failing to register as a foreign agent under the Federal Law on Non-Commercial Organizations» ('OSCE PA's Human Rights Chair Criticizes Russia's Targeting of Sakharov Centre', OSCE Parliamentary Assembly [website], 2015).

45. G. Revzin, *Ochen' vazhnyy marshrut. Malyye muzei Moskvy*, Izdatelskie Resheniya, Moscow, 2017, p. 22.

46. V. Dubina, 2019, op. cit., p. 326.

47. See the declaration of the GULAG History State Museum concerning the *Concept of State Policy on the Memorialization of the Victims of Political Repression* signed by the then president D. Medvedev in August 2015 ('Concept of the State Policy', GULAG History Museum [website], 2020).

48. R. Romanov cited in Architectural Council of Moscow, 2015, op. cit.

49. K. Sokol, 'Ot kritiki muzeya k yego emansipatsii', Colta.ru [website], 14 November 2016.

50. M. Iampolski, 2018, op. cit., pp. 62-63.

51. R. Romanov cited in L. Lunina, 'Mesto lisheniya nesvobody', *Ogoniok*, no. 15, 2016, p. 32.

52. The head of the president's administration A. Vaino is the Boris Yeltsin Presidential Center NGO board chairman (E. Boltunova, 'The President Has Entered the Building! The Boris Yeltsin Presidential Center and Memorial Tradition in Contemporary Russia', *Ab Imperio*, vol. 3, 2017, p. 178). In 2015, T. Yumasheva stated: «It is not only a private family matter but also a matter of the state. The president, the prime minister and the president's administration always helped us and responded to all our requests» (cited in J. Taratuta, 'Tatyana

Yumasheva: 'Mify prizhilis', i s nimi ochen' trudno borotsya'', Forbes [website], 22 October 2015).

53. E. Boltunova, 2017, op. cit., p. 169.

54. D. Sudjic, *The Edifice Complex: How the Rich and Powerful Shape the World*, Allen Lane, London, 2005, pp. 2, 7-8.

55. C. Whitehead, 2016, op. cit., p. 3.

56. T. Bennett, 'The Exhibitionary Complex', *New Formations*, no. 4, 1988, pp. 73-102; T. Bennett, 1995, op. cit.

57. S. Macdonald, 2012, op. cit.; S. Macdonald, 2013, op. cit.

58. Eng. "transmitter of cultural values".

59. See, for instance, various public opinions on the 1939 Molotov-Ribbentrop Pact (official name: *Treaty of Non-Aggression between Germany and the Union of Soviet Socialist Republics*) recently expressed by V. Putin. Thus, during the CIS summit in December 2019, Putin stated: «The Soviet Union never took anything from Poland» (cited in 'Vladimir Putin Wants to Rehabilitate Stalin's Pact with Hitler', The Economist [website], 23 January 2020). These opinions provoked an adverse reaction of both the Polish authorities (Ministry of Foreign Affairs – Republic of Poland, 'Statement of Polish MFA on False Narratives Presented by the Russian Federation', Ministry of Foreign Affairs – Republic of Poland [website], 21 December 2019) and European political leaders, triggering a political crisis between Russia and Poland.

60. A. Applebaum, 'Putin's Big Lie', The Atlantic [website], 5 January 2020.

61. During the press conference in December 2019, Putin claimed: «I know about the European Parliament's decision. I consider it absolutely unacceptable and wrong, because you can condemn Stalinism and totalitarianism as a whole, and in some ways, these will be well-deserved reproaches. Our people were the biggest victims of totalitarianism. We condemned it and the personality cult and so on. But to equate the Soviet Union or to put the Soviet Union and Nazi Germany on one level is incredible cynicism» (cited in President of Russia, 'Vladimir Putin's Annual News Conference', President of Russia [website], 19 December 2019).

62. The author is using the phrase coined by J. Stalin in his 1930 article 'Dizzy with Success: Concerning Questions of the Collective-Farm Movement' (see, for instance, in R. D. Markwick, *Rewriting History in Soviet Russia: The Politics of Revisionist Historiography, 1956–1974*,

Palgrave, Basingstoke and New York, 2001, p. 141), which has become a commonly used Russian term for describing the intention to minimize the impact of political crimes committed by the state authorities.

Bibliography

- Abzalova, E., 'El Centro Conmemorativo de la Historia de la Represión Política 'Perm-36', in Alonso, M., ed., *El Lugar de la Memoria: La Huella del Mal Como Pedagogía Democrática*, Bakeaz, Bilbao, 2012, pp. 69-94.
- Applebaum, A., 'Putin's Big Lie', The Atlantic [website], 5 January 2020.
- Architectural Council of Moscow, 'Arkhitekturnyy proyekt dlya Muzeya GULAGa', Architectural Council of Moscow [website], 10 June 2015.
- Assmann, A., *Zeit und Tradition: kulturelle Strategien der Dauer*, Böhlau, Cologne, 1999.
- — *Erinnerungsräume: Formen und Wandlungen des kulturellen Gedächtnisses*, 2nd ed., C.H. Beck, Munich, 2003 [1999].
- — 'Response to Peter Novick', *Bulletin of the German Historical Institute*, no. 40, 2007, pp. 33-38.
- — *Das neue Unbehagen an der Erinnerungskultur: Eine Intervention*, C.H. Beck, Munich, 2013.
- — *Shadows of Trauma: Memory and the Politics of Postwar Identity*, trans. by S. Clift, Fordham University Press, New York, 2016.
- Assmann, J., *Das Kulturelle Gedächtnis: Schrift, Erinnerung und Politische Identität in frühen Hochkulturen*, C.H. Beck, Munich, 1992.
- — *Religion and Cultural Memory: Ten Studies*, trans. by R. Livingstone, Stanford University Press, Stanford, 2006.
- Basso Peressut, L., *Il Museo Moderno: Architettura e museografia da Auguste Perret a Louis I. Kahn*, Edizioni Lybra Immagine, Milan, 2005.
- Bennett, T., 'The Exhibitionary Complex', *New Formations*, no. 4, 1988, pp. 73-102.
- — *The Birth of the Museum: History, Theory, Politics*, Routledge, London and New York, 1995.

- Bogumil, Z., *Gulag Memories: The Rediscovery and Commemoration of Russia's Repressive Past*, Berghahn Books, Oxford and New York, 2018.
- Boltunova, E., 'The President Has Entered the Building! The Boris Yeltsin Presidential Center and Memorial Tradition in Contemporary Russia', *Ab Imperio*, vol. 3, 2017, pp. 165-193.
- Brooker, G., & Stone, S., *Re-readings: Interior Architecture and the Design Principles of Remodelling Existing Buildings*, RIBA Enterprises, London, 2004.
- Burke, P., 'History as Social Memory', in Butler, T., ed., *Memory: History, Culture, and the Mind*, Blackwell, Oxford, 1989, pp. 97-113.
- Cento Bull, A. & Hansen, H. L., 'On Agonistic Memory', *Memory Studies*, vol. 9, no. 4, 2015, pp. 390-404.
- Chaadaev, P. Y., *Polnoe sobranie sochineniy i izbrannye pis'ma*, vol. 1, Nauka, Moscow, 1991 [1829], pp. 320-339.
- Chechel, I., 'Daniil Dondurei: 'Sverhtsennosti' opiat' ostanavlivaiyt Rossiyu? Rossiiskaya gosudarstvennost': k etiologii sverhtsennostei, Gefter [website], 2 February 2015.
- Conquest, R., *The Great Terror: A Reassessment*, Pimlico, London, 2008 [1968].
- De Cesari, C. & Rigney, A., 'Introduction', in De Cesari, C. & Rigney, A., eds, *Transnational Memory: Circulation, Articulation, Scales*, De Gruyter, Berlin, 2014, pp. 1-25.
- Dobritsina, I. A., *Ot postmodernizma − k nelineynoy arkhitekture. Arkhitektura v kontekste sovremennoy filosofii*, Progress-Tradiziya, Moscow, 2004.
- Drugman, F., 'Il museo diffuso', *Hinterland*, no. 21-22, 1982, pp. 24-25.
- Dubina, V., 'Virtualnoye mesto pamyati i realnoye prostranstvo GULAGa v sovremennoy Rossii', in Zavadsky, A., Sklez, V. & Suverina, K., eds, *Politika affekta: muzej kak prostranstvo publichnoj istorii*, Novoye literaturnoe obozrenie, Moscow, 2019, pp. 320-336.
- Eder, J. S., *Holocaust Angst: The Federal Republic of Germany and American Holocaust Memory since the 1970s*, Oxford University Press, Oxford and New York, 2016.
- Erll, A. & Rigney, A., eds, *Mediation, Remediation, and the Dynamics of Cultural Memory*, Walter de Gruyter, Berlin and

95

New York, 2009, pp. 1-11.

- Etkind, A., *Internal Colonization: Russia's Imperial Experience*, Polity Press, Cambridge and Malden, 2011.

- — *Warped Mourning: Stories of the Undead in the Land of the Unburied*, Stanford University Press, Stanford, 2013.

- Etkind, A. et al., *Remembering Katyn*, Polity Press, Cambridge and Malden, 2012.

- 'Federal Law no. 68-FZ 'O tsentrakh istoricheskogo naslediia prezidentov Rossiyskoy Federatsii, prekrativshikh ispolnenie svoikh polnomochiy', *Sobraniye Zakonodatelstva RF*, no. 20/2253, 13 May 2008.

- 'Federal Law no. 125-FZ 'O svobode sovesti i o religioznykh objedineniyakh', *Sobraniye Zakonodatelstva RF*, no. 39/4465, 26 September 1997.

- Federal State Statistics Service, *Rossiya v tsifrakh 2017: kratkiy statisticheskiy sbornik*, Moscow, 2017.

- Foer, J. S., *Everything Is Illuminated*, Houghton Mifflin, New York, 2002.

- Garden, M.-C., 'The Heritagescape: Looking at Landscapes of the Past', *International Journal of Heritage Studies*, vol. 12, no. 5, 2006, pp. 394-411.

- Gessen, M., 'How Arseny Roginsky Confronted the Politics of Memory in Russia', The New Yorker [website], 19 December 2017.

- Gololobov, I., 'The Soviet People: The Rise and Fall of an Ideological Federalism', in Kavalski, E. & Zolkos, M., eds, *Defunct Federalisms: Critical Perspectives on Federal Failure*, Ashgate Publishing, Farnham and Burlington, 2008, pp. 145-156.

- Gorelik, G. & Bouis, A. W., *The World of Andrei Sakharov: A Russian Physicist's Path to Freedom*, Oxford University Press, Oxford and New York, 2005.

- GULAG History Museum, 'Concept of the State Policy', GULAG History Museum [website], 2020.

- Gurianov, A. E., Raczynski, A. & Zenkevich, A., *Ubity v Katyni: Kniga pamyati polskikh voyennoplennykh – uznikov Kozelskogo lagerya NKVD, rasstrelyannykh po resheniyu Politbyuro TSK VKP(b) ot 5 marta 1940 goda*, Memorial NGO/Zvenya, Moscow, 2015.

- Habermas, J., 'A Kind of Settlement of Damages (Apologetic

Tendencies)', trans. by J. Leaman, *New German Critique*, no. 44, 1988 [1986], pp. 25-39.

- Halbwachs, M., *On Collective Memory,* The University of Chicago Press, London and Chicago, 1992 [1950].

- Hirsch, M., *Family Frames: Photography, Narrative, and Postmemory*, Harvard University Press, Cambridge, 1997.

- — *The Generation of Postmemory: Writing and Visual Culture After the Holocaust*, Columbia University Press, New York, 2012.

- Hufbauer, B., *Presidential Temples: How Memorials and Libraries Shape Public Memory*, University Press of Kansas, Lawrence, 2005.

- Huyssen, A., 'The Voids of Berlin', *Critical Inquiry*, vol. 24, no. 1, 1997, pp. 57-81.

- Iampolski, M., *Park Kultury: Kultura i nasilie v Moskve segodnya*, Novoe Izdatelstvo, Moscow, 2018.

- International Coalition of Sites of Conscience, 'Gulag Museum at Perm-36 (Russia)', International Coalition of Sites of Conscience [website], 2019.

- Ivanova, G. M., *Istoriya GULAGa, 1918–1958: sotsialno-ekonomicheskiy i politiko-pravovoy aspekty*, Nauka, Moscow, 2006.

- Kaulen, M. E., ed., *Muzeyefikatsiya istoriko-kulturnogo naslediya Rossii*, Eterna, Moscow, 2012.

- Khapaeva, D., 'Historical Memory in Post-Soviet Gothic Society', *Social Research*, vol. 76, no. 1, 2009, pp. 359-394.

- *Konstitutsiia Rossiiskoi Federatsii: Ofitsialnoe izdanie*, Yuridicheskaya Literatura, Moscow, 2005 [1993].

- Koposov, N., *Memory Laws, Memory Wars: The Politics of the Past in Europe and Russia*, Cambridge University Press, Cambridge, 2017.

- Koselleck, R., 'Forms and Traditions of Negative Memory' [Formen und Traditionen des negativen Gedächtnisses], in Knigge, V. & Frei, N., eds, *Verbrechen erinnern: Die Auseinandersetzung mit Holocaust und Völkermord,* C.H. Beck, Munich, 2002, pp. 21-32.

- Laarse, R. van der, 'Beyond Auschwitz? Europe's Terrorscapes in the Age of Postmemory', in Silberman, M. & Vatan, F., eds, *Memory and Postwar Memorials: Confronting the Violence of the Past*, Palgrave Macmillan, New York, 2013, pp. 71-92.

- — '"Ils nous l'ont fait": Muséographie des mémoires concurrents après 1989', in Bechtel, D. & Jurgenson, L., eds, *Muséographie des violences en Europe centrale et ex-URSS*, Editions Kimé, Paris, 2016, pp. 213-232.

- Laarse, R. van der, Mazzucchelli, F. & Reijnen, C., 'Introduction: Traces of Terror, Signs of Trauma', in Laarse, R. van der, Mazzucchelli, F. & Reijnen, C., eds, *'Traces of Terror, Signs of Trauma': Practices of (Re)Presentation of Collective Memories in Space in Contemporary Europe (VS Versus, no. 119)*, Bompiani, Milano, 2014, pp. 3-19.

- Lanzmann, C. & Gantheret, F., 'Les non-lieux de la mémoire', *Nouvelle Revue de Psychanalyse*, vol. 33, 1986, pp. 11-24.

- Lehrer, E., Milton, C. E. & Patterson, M. E., eds, *Curating Difficult Knowledge: Violent Pasts in Public Places*, Palgrave Macmillan, New York, 2011.

- Levin, M. D., *The Modern Museum: Temple or Showroom*, Dvir Publishing House, Tel Aviv, 1983.

- Lübbe, H., *Der Fortschritt und das Museum. Über den Grund unseres Vergnügens an historischen Gegenständen*, Institute of Germanic Studies, London, 1982.

- Lunina, L., 'Mesto lisheniya nesvobody', *Ogoniok*, no. 15, 2016, p. 32.

- Macdonald, S., 'Theorizing Museums: An Introduction', in Macdonald, S. & Fyfe, G., eds, *Theorizing Museums: Representing Identity and Diversity in a Changing World*, Blackwell, Oxford, 1996, pp. 1-18.

- — 'Unsettling Memories: Intervention and Controversy over Difficult Public Heritage', in Anico, M. & Peralta, E., eds, *Heritage and Identity. Engagement and Demission in the Contemporary World*, Routledge, London and New York, 2008, pp. 93-104.

- — *Difficult Heritage: Negotiating the Nazi Past in Nuremberg and Beyond*, Routledge, London and New York, 2009.

- — 'Presencing Europe's Pasts', in Kockel, U., Craith, M. N. & Frykman, J., eds, *A Companion to the Anthropology of Europe*, Wiley-Blackwell, Chichester, 2012, pp. 233-252.

- — *Memorylands: Heritage and Identity in Europe Today*, Routledge, London and New York, 2013.

- Macleod, S., Hourston Hanks, L. & Hale, J., eds, *Museum*

Making: Narratives, Architectures, Exhibitions, Routledge, London and New York, 2012.

- Maistrovskaya, M. T., *Muzey kak obyekt kultury: iskusstvo ekspozitsionnogo ansamblya*, Progress-Tradiziya, Moscow, 2015.

- Markwick, R. D., *Rewriting History in Soviet Russia: The Politics of Revisionist Historiography, 1956–1974*, Palgrave, Basingstoke and New York, 2001.

- Memorial NGO Perm Branch, *Memorialnyy muzey istorii politicheskikh repressiy i totalitarizma. Kuchino (Permskaya oblast'). Otchot 1994/1995*, Memorial NGO Perm Branch/Perm Region Administration/Sotzium, Perm, 1996.

- Menon, R. & Rumer, E., *Conflict in Ukraine: The Unwinding of the Post-Cold War Order*, The MIT Press, Cambridge and London, 2015.

- Message, K., *New Museums and the Making of Culture*, Berg, Oxford and New York, 2006.

- Mikaelyan, M., *Dissonant Memories in the Post-Soviet Space: Newly Established Museums and Political History in Russia (1991–2016), Appendixes,* PhD diss., Politecnico di Milano, Milan, 2020.

- Miller, A. & Lipman, M., eds, *Istoricheskaya politika v XXI veke*, Novoye literaturnoe obozrenie, Moscow, 2012.

- Ministry of Culture of the Russian Federation, 'Memorialnyy kompleks Katyn' budet dostroyen', Ministry of Culture of the Russian Federation [website], 7 August 2017.

- Ministry of Foreign Affairs – Republic of Poland, 'Statement of Polish MFA on False Narratives Presented by the Russian Federation', Ministry of Foreign Affairs – Republic of Poland [website], 21 December 2019.

- Nora, P., ed., *Les lieux de mémoire*, Gallimard, Paris, 1984–1992.

- — 'Between Memory and History: Les Lieux de Mémoire', trans. by M. Roudebush, *Representations*, no. 26, 1989, pp. 7-24.

- Nuttall, M., 'Memoryscape: A Sense of Locality in Northwest Greenland', *North Atlantic Studies*, vol. 1, no. 2, 1991, pp. 39-50.

- Olick, J. K., *The Politics of Regret: On Collective Memory and Historical* Responsibility, Routledge, London and New York, 2007.

- Olick, J. K. & Robbins, J., 'Social Memory Studies: From

'Collective Memory' to the Historical Sociology of Mnemonic Practices', *Annual Review of Sociology*, vol. 24, 1998, pp. 105-140.

- OSCE Parliamentary Assembly, 'OSCE PA's Human Rights Chair Criticises Russia's Targeting of Sakharov Centre', OSCE Parliamentary Assembly [website], 2015.

- Paramonova, D., Griby, mutanty i drugiye: arkhitektura ery Luzhkova, Strelka Press, Moscow, 2013.

- Parthé, K., 'Russia's 'Unreal Estate': Cognitive Mapping and National Identity', *Kennan Institute Occasional Papers*, vol. 267, 1997, pp. 1-30.

- Perm-36 Memorial Museum-Reserve of the History of Political Repression, 'Otchet o vypolnenii gosudarstvennogo zadaniya no. 466 na 2018 god', Perm-36 Memorial Museum-Reserve of the History of Political Repression [website], 11 January 2019.

- Pobol, N. L. & Polyan, P. M., *Stalinskie deportatsii: 1928–1953*, MFD/Materik, Moscow, 2005.

- Pollack, M., *Kontaminierte Landschaften: Unruhe bewahren*, Residenz Verlag, St. Pölten, 2014.

- Polyan, P. M., *Istoriomor, ili trepanatsiya pamyati: Bitvy za pravdu o GULAGe, deportatsiyakh, voyne i Kholokoste*, AST, Moscow, 2016.

- Proshansky, H. M., Fabian, A. K. & Kaminoff, R., 'Place-identity: Physical World Socialization of the Self', *Journal of Environmental Psychology*, vol. 3. no. 1, 1983, pp. 57-83.

- Ralph Appelbaum Associates, 'Jewish Museum and Tolerance Center', Ralph Appelbaum Associates [website], 2019.

- Revzin, G., 'Repressii v naturalnuyu velichinu: Muzey istorii GULAGa', *Kommersant Weekend*, no. 30, 2009, p. 16.

- — *Russkaya arkhitektura rubezha XX–XXI vv.*, Novoye Izdatelstvo, Moscow, 2013.

- — *Ochen' vazhnyy marshrut. Malyye muzei Moskvy*, Izdatelskie Resheniya, Moscow, 2017.

- RIA Novosti, 'Vystuplenie Vladimira Putina na mitinge v Luzhnikah', RIA Novosti [website], 23 February 2012.

- Rose, J., *Interpreting Difficult History at Museums and Historic Sites*, Rowman & Littlefield, Lanham, 2016.

- Sabanchiev, H.-M. A., *Byli soslany navechno: Deportatsiya i reabilitatsiya balkarskogo naroda*, Elbrus, Nalchik, 2004.

- Scherrer, J., 'Russlands neue-alte Erinnerungsorte', *Aus Politik und Zeitgeschichte*, no. 11, 2006, pp. 24-28.
- Sendyka, R., 'The Difficult Heritage of Non-Sites of Memory: Contested Places, Contaminated Landscapes', *TRACES Journal*, vol. 3, 2017, pp. 4-15.
- Shmyrov, V., 'The Gulag Museum', *Museum International*, vol. 53, no. 1, 2001, pp. 25-27.
- — 'Perm-36'. Reabilitatsiya repressiy, Memorial NGO Perm Regional Branch [website], 2016.
- Sindbæk Andersen, T. & Törnquist-Plewa, B., 'Introduction: Disputed Memories in Central, Eastern and South-Eastern Europe', in Sindbæk Andersen, T. & Törnquist-Plewa, B., eds, *Disputed Memory: Emotions and Memory Politics in Central, Eastern and South-Eastern Europe*, De Gruyter, Berlin, 2016, pp. 1-17.
- Sniegon, T., 'A Transformation of the Memorial Site in Katyn', PONARS Eurasia [website], 14 June 2019.
- Sokol, K., 'Ot kritiki muzeya k yego emansipatsii', Colta.ru [website], 14 November 2016.
- Sudjic, D., *The Edifice Complex: How the Rich and Powerful Shape the World*, Allen Lane, London, 2005.
- Svanidze, N., 'Hard Day's Night: Nikolai Svanidze' [video recording], TV Rain [website], 4 May 2017.
- Taratuta, J., 'Tatyana Yumasheva: 'Mify prizhilis', i s nimi ochen' trudno borotsya', Forbes [website], 22 October 2015.
- Tumarkin, M., *Traumascapes: The Power and Fate of Places Transformed by Tragedy*, Melbourne University Press, Melbourne, 2005.
- Tunbridge, J. E. & Ashworth, G. J., *Dissonant Heritage: The Management of the Past as a Resource in Conflict*, John Wiley & Sons, Chichester, 1995.
- Tzortzi, K., *Museum Space: Where Architecture Meets Museology*, Routledge, London and New York, 2015.
- United Nations, 'Russian Federation: Country Profile. Implementation of Agenda 21: Review of Progress Made Since the United Nations Conference on Environment and Development', United Nations [website], December 1996.
- VCIOM, 'Stalinskie repressii: prestuplenie ili nakazanie?', VCIOM [website], 5 July 2017.

- — 'Politicheskiye presledovaniya 30–40 gg. XX veka: motivy i maschtaby', VCIOM [website], 2 October 2017.
- Viola, L., *The Unknown Gulag: The Lost World of Stalin's Special Settlements*, Oxford University Press, Oxford and New York, 2009.
- Violi, P., 'Trauma Site Museums and Politics of Memory', *Theory, Culture & Society*, vol. 29, no. 1, 2012, pp. 36-75.
- 'Vladimir Putin Wants to Rehabilitate Stalin's Pact with Hitler', The Economist [website], 23 January 2020.
- Vlasik, A., Yesipchuk, M. & Napreenko, G., 'Chto ne tak s novym Muzeyem istorii GULAGa', Colta.ru [website], 7 November 2016.
- Whitehead, C., 'Critical Analysis Tool (CAT): Why Analyze Museum Display?', Digital Cultures in Culture Lab, Newcastle University [website], 2016.
- Whitehead, C. et al., eds, *'Placing' Europe in the Museum: People(s), Places, Identities*, Politecnico di Milano, Milan, 2013.
- Williams, P., *Memorial Museums: The Global Rush to Commemorate Atrocities*, Berg, Oxford and New York, 2007.
- — 'The Memorial Museum Identity Complex: Victimhood, Culpability, and Responsibility', in Carbonell, B. M., ed., *Museum Studies: An Anthology of Contexts*, Blackwell, Oxford, 2012, pp. 97-115.
- — 'Treading Difficult Ground: The Effort to Establish Russia's First National Gulag Museum', in Poulot, D., Lanzarote Guiral, J. M. & Bodenstein, F., eds, *National Museums and the Negotiation of Difficult Pasts [EuNaMus Report, no. 8]*, Linköping University Electronic Press, Linköping, 2012, pp. 111-121.
- Witcomb, A., *Re-Imagining the Museum: Beyond the Mausoleum*, Routledge, London and New York, 2003.
- Yurshina, M., 'Roman Romanov, direktor muzeya istorii GULAGa: "Repressirovannym bol'she vsego nuzhno priznaniye obshchestva"', Istoricheskaya pamyat': XX vek [website], 1 January 2013.
- Zhegulev, I., '"Ya schital sebya otvetstvennym za Putina". Peryemnika Yeltsina privela k vlasti 'sem'ya', Meduza [website], 11 March 2019.

Bronze model of the *Worker and Kolkhoz Woman* sculpture by V. Mukhina. Source: M. Mikaelyan (2020).

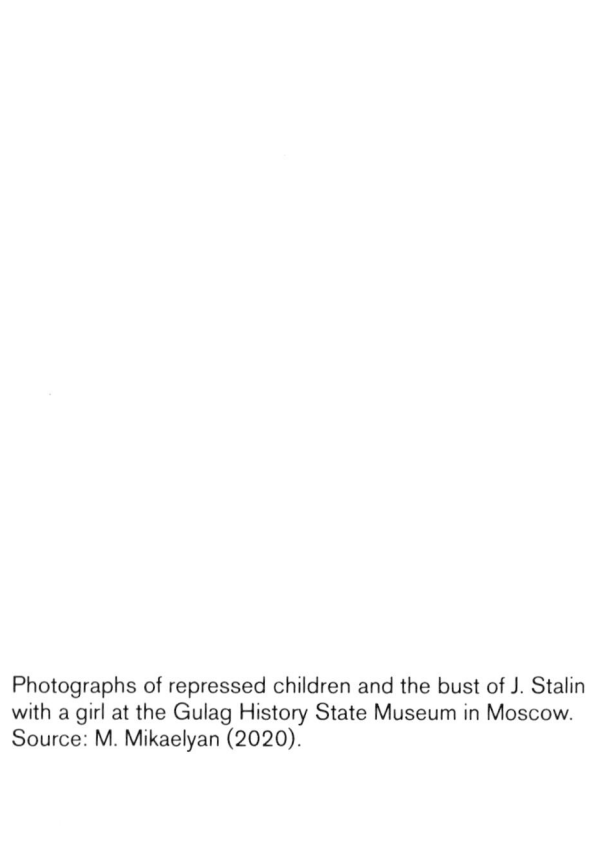

Photographs of repressed children and the bust of J. Stalin with a girl at the Gulag History State Museum in Moscow. Source: M. Mikaelyan (2020).

Auid Series:

01
Francesca Zanotto
Circular Architecture

02
Claudia Zanda
The Architecture of a Motorway

03
Maria Mikaelyan
The Museum as a Political Instrument

04
Gerardo Semprebon
Rural Futures